THE CASE OF

THE PAINTED BICYCLE LAMP

COVENTRY'S UNSOLVED DOUBLE MURDER OF 1906

ADAM WOOD
author of The Watchmaker's Revenge

40/50

Published by

Mango Books
18 Soho Square
London
W1D 3QL

For information on author talks and signings visit
www.BicycleLampBook.com

ISBN: 978-1-914277-375

THE CASE OF

THE PAINTED BICYCLE LAMP

For Mary and Richard Phillips,
in memory of their blissful eighteen months.

ACKNOWLEDGEMENTS

Following the publication of my book *The Watchmaker's Revenge* – the incredible story of Oliver Style's rampage through the streets of Victorian Coventry with a loaded revolver – several local readers asked me what the follow-up would be. After all, they said, there's a lot of history in Coventry; there must be further dark tales to be unearthed. I subsequently spent a day trawling the British Newspaper Archive for such stories, and I can report that there are indeed a great number.

The Case of the Painted Bicycle Lamp tells the story of one of them, and, as is always the case, several people provided information, help and encouragement as I pieced together the links in the chain (pun intended).

My grateful thanks, then, are due to Frank Barnes; Corinne Brazier; Keith Bushnell; Malvern Carvell; David Fry; Nikki Hagan; Jo Phillips; Lucy Rackliff; Mark Ripper; Paul Sheehan; Phil Tutchings; Coventry Archives; the knowledgeable members of the Visit Historic Coventry Facebook page; the staff at Stoke Library; members of the Stoke Park Residents Group and the Stoke Local History Group; Lesley Martin of Coventry Libraries; Rob Orland of the fantastic HistoricCoventry.co.uk website; Helen Taylor, Museum Manager of the West Midlands Police Museum; Ian Woolley, Chairman of the Friends of London Road Cemetery; and Mrs Wood. My special thanks to Kevin Malcolm and John Marshall, who generously shared their vast knowledge of Stoke's history and supplied unique images of the area.

Thank you all.

Adam Wood
Coventry, 13 June 2022

ABOUT THE AUTHOR

Adam Wood is the author of *The Watchmaker's Revenge*, an account of the long-forgotten shooting rampage in Victorian Coventry by Oliver Style, set against the backdrop of the vibrant watchmaking community of the 1840s-1880s. He offers lectures and a walking tour of sites assocated with the story.

Adam is also the author of *Swanson: The Life and Times of a Victorian Detective*, a detailed biography of the detective who was in charge of the investigation into the Jack the Ripper murders from Scotland Yard, and *Trial of Percy Lefroy Mapleton*, an examination of the notorious 1881 railway murder of Frederick Gold on the London to Brighton express. He is also co-author with Police historian Neil Bell of *Sir Howard Vincent's Police Code, 1889*, and a series of historic walking guidebooks with Blue Badge tour guide Richard Jones.

Adam is Executive Editor of *Ripperologist* magazine, the leading publication dedicated to the serious study of the Whitechapel murders and their place in social history. From 2017 to 2021 he was Editor of the *Journal* of the Police History Society.

www.AdamWoodAuthor.com

THE CASE OF THE
PAINTED BICYCLE LAMP

Stoke Park in 1903.

Author's collection.

A CYCLE LAMP
HAS BEEN FOUND

"There is little light upon the double murder at Stoke. There have been supposed clues, and they have been followed up without success. The Police are continuing their investigations with unabated vigour, and it is not of course impossible that they may discover the murderer, but so far the grounds of hope are not substantial.

The whole thing is shrouded in mystery. A fearful crime was committed, and the murderer of an old man and woman so well concealed his traces that he left nothing behind upon which the Police could formulate a plan.

A cycle lamp has been found in the kitchen of the house which is thought to belong to the assassin, and the most is being made of this. But there are hundreds and thousands of cycle lamps even in Coventry, and there is nothing specially distinctive about it. Still it is something, and may yet form an important piece of evidence."

'The Stoke Murder: Mystery Unsolved.'
Coventry Herald, 27 January 1906.

*

The best detective stories always seem to have a memorable prop central to the narrative. Conan Doyle gave Sherlock Holmes the speckled band, five orange pips and more; Agatha Christie's Miss Marple quite literally had a body in the library.

While in no way attempting to place this story anywhere even *near* the same bracket as those great writers, this true story has a similar device – a battered, blackened bicycle lamp, of no real value to anyone, but which proved to be the object which helped Coventry's City Police build their case against their prime suspect; an object which they were willing to use in an attempt to send him to the gallows.

As the *Coventry Herald* reporter says on the previous page, there were innumerable bicycle lamps in the city in 1906. But only one was found in the home of Richard and Mary Phillips following their horrible deaths, and this entered into evidence as the Stoke Lamp. It was, therefore, a very special lamp indeed.

*

There are forty-two deaths related in this book, including two murders, two suicides, one horrific accidental death, and ten instances of infant mortality.

Despite this, at its heart this is a story of two kind, generous people who had but eighteen months together, after leading long lives elsewhere. They met late in life, but both enjoyed the happiest time of their long lives following their marriage in 1904.

But, as is always the case with history, their pasts coloured their future together. Both suffered loss, both spouses and children, which no doubt made the brief time they enjoyed together all the sweeter.

It is also the story of a changing city. As the story unfolded with my ongoing research, a picture emerged of the ever-developing industries of Coventry; Richard Phillips, the male victim, was a retired watchmaker, and Mary, his wife, came from a family steeped in the textile industry. Her first husband was prominent in the city's bicycle trade, while Richard's sons later forged a career in the burgeoning motor industry.

To understand the Stoke Park murders and the victims in their proper context, we need to take a look at which was happening in Coventry in the years leading up to the turn of the Twentieth century – starting right back at the 1830s.

1.
MARY AND ROBERT

Although the story of the Stoke Park murders takes place to the east of Coventry, it very much has its beginnings on the other side of the city, where the early industries of textiles and watchmaking were focussed.

While the victims may have been in the late autumn of their lives by the time of their deaths, they had, of course, both enjoyed middle age, youth and childhood.

Mary Taylor was born at Spon Street to Joseph, a silk dyer, and his wife Mary on 5 June 1836. A non-conformist family, Mary was one of twenty children baptised at a public event at the independent Vicar Lane Chapel on 21 August that year.[1]

The chapel had been established in 1724, and was one of several independent places of worship around the city. After a slow beginning, the congregation grew over the years and in 1822 the chapel was enlarged to accommodate 1,200 worshippers; at the same time rooms were opened on Spon Street and Much Park Street to allow weekday meetings. Three years before Mary was born, the Chapel had added schoolrooms for Sunday and week-day education,[2] and it is likely that Mary attended in her early years.

---

1   Non–Conformist and Non–Parochial Registers, 1567-1936, Piece 2980: Coventry, Vicar Lane (Independent), 1806-1837.

2   The number of worshippers remained steady, and in 1891 a new chapel was opened in Warwick Road. The chapel and schoolrooms at Vicar Lane were sold in 1897, and the building destroyed in an air raid in 1941. ['The City of Coventry: Protestant nonconformity, Places of worship' in *A History of the County of Warwick: Volume 8, the City of Coventry and Borough of Warwick* (1969).]

Sovereign Place, where the Taylor family were living
at the time of daughter Ann's death

The family were living on Butts Lane in 1841, when the census was taken, and it's interesting to note that of their neighbours there was an even division of those employed in textile work such as weaving and dyeing, and people engaged in the watchmaking industry, which was just beginning to take off in Coventry.[3]

Another daughter, Ann, had been born earlier that year,[4] but sadly did not survive for long. Just eighteen months later she died at the then family home on Sovereign Place, off the Butts, and was buried at St Michael's, Coventry, on 22 November 1842.[5]

By the age of fourteen Mary was working alongside her mother and father in textiles at their home on Sovereign Place, Mary as silk worker, Joseph a silk dyer and Mary Sr a silk winder.[6] Ten years later they were still working together, with Mary, now twenty–four years old, having progressed to silk winding. The family had moved

3   1841 Census.
4   Ann Taylor is recorded as being four months old when the census was taken, on 6 June 1841.
5   Church of England Burials: Coventry, St Michael 1825-1849.
6   1851 Census.

back to Butts Lane, this time No. 56. Of the row of six houses in which they were situated, the Taylors were the only family fully engaged in weaving; the rest had moved into watchmaking, which was approaching its peak years.[7]

It was a familiar story ten years later; still at 56 Butts Lane, Joseph was a silk dyer, Mary Sr a silk winder, and their daughter now a frilling corder. Around them were watch finishers, a watch case maker, a watch pinion maker and a watch balance maker.[8]

Further along the Butts, first at Junction Street[9] and then York Street,[10] were Joseph's brother William and his family. Although not especially close, the families did share the way they earned their living; William was, like his brother, a silk dyer, and his wife Sarah was a silk winder. William's son Robert Taylor – Mary's cousin – found himself in trouble when he was found to be drinking in the Albion Tavern on nearby Thomas Street at a quarter to midnight, when the inn should have been closed. Robert, who was earning a living as a carpenter, was brought before the magistrates with fellow drinker James Lawrenson, a watchmaker, and after both promised not to do it again they were fined 5s with costs.[11]

But for Mary, things were about to change. Although past the first blush of youth, she had, at the age of thirty-four, met her future husband.

*

Robert Seymour Waterfall not only enjoyed a spectacular name, but he too came from a family of non-Christian worshippers. His father, Edmund Waterfall, was one of eleven children born to John Waterfall and Sarah Cash, both from a long line of Coventry Quakers.[12]

---

7   1861 Census.
8   1871 Census.
9   1851 Census.
10 1861 Census.
11 *Coventry Herald*, 1 October 1875.
12 John Waterfall and Sarah Cash were married on 30 January 1794, at a quarterly meeting of Leicestershire and Rutland Quakers held in Coventry. [Piece 0989: Quarterly Meeting of Warwickshire, Leicestershire and Rutland: Marriages (1729-1794).]

Edmund Waterfall married Libra Jephcott on 5 June 1832 at St Lawrence, Foleshill,[13] and the couple soon welcomed daughter Ann.[14] A son, Edmund Jr, was born two years later.[15] A commercial clerk, Edmund then took the family to London, and son Robert was born there in Bermondsey, south of the river, in 1837. Sadly, the exact date is unrecorded.

In 1841 the family were living on Philip Lane, by London Wall,[16] and welcomed another daughter, Mary, there in 1842. Tragically, eldest son Edmund Jr died on 31 January 1845, just nine years old. Later that year the arrival of another son, George, went some way to mending their broken hearts.[17] In 1851 the Waterfalls were still in Bermondsey, at 8 St James Place, with the surviving children all receiving an education.[18]

But by the time of the next census, on 7 April 1861, everything had changed. The Waterfall family were back in Foleshill, living at 'The White House' on Brick Kiln Lane.[19] Father Edmund, now fifty–five, was working as a commercial clerk for a ribbon warehouse, with sons Robert (now twenty–four) and George (sixteen) employed as ribbon warehousemen – quite probably the same premises.

By 1871 the family were at 19 Spon Street. Edmund was still employed as a clerk, with Robert working as a warehouseman. With mother Libra now seventy years old, Ann had taken over housekeeping duties.[20]

George Waterfall had not only left home, but had also changed his vocation; now twenty–seven, he was a farmer at Exhall, and married Amelia Falconbridge on 26 October that year at Allesley

---

13   Marriage record of Edmund Waterfall and Libra Jephcott.
14   Ann Atkins Waterfall was born on 20 October 1833 and baptised 20 September 1835. [Independent and Some Baptist, Foleshill, Warwick, England. FHL Film Number: 825430.]
15   On 26 April 1835. [Private information from descendants of Thomas Cash].
16   1841 Census.
17   Dates from private information given by descendants of Thomas Cash.
18   1851 Census.
19   Now Broad Street.
20   1871 Census.

St John the Baptist, Spon Street,
where Robert Waterfall married Mary Taylor in 1871
Courtesy www.historiccoventry.co.uk

Parish Church.[21]

It was to be the first of two weddings celebrated by the family within a matter of months. On Christmas Day, 1871, Robert Seymour Waterfall waited at the end of the aisle of St John the Baptist on Spon Street for his new wife, Mary Taylor. Both bride and groom were thirty-four years old; she was living on the Butts at the time of the marriage, he on Spon Street itself.[22]

Soon after their marriage they moved from the Spon Street area to 58 Howard Street, to the north of the city centre, and Robert is listed in trade directories of the 1870s there was a storekeeper.[23]

---

21 Marriage record of George Waterfall and Amelia Falconbridge.
22 Marriage record of Robert Seymour Waterfall and Mary Taylor.
23 *1874 White's Directory and Gazeteer of Warwickshire; 1875 White & Co.'s Commercial & Trades Directory of Birmingham.*

A daughter, Ellen, was born at home on 5 April 1873,[24] and no doubt the Waterfalls looked to a happy future; but a period of tragedy lay ahead.

On 15 September 1875, with Ellen two and a half years old, her grandfather Joseph Taylor died at his home – 56 Butts – after a long period suffering with kidney and bladder disease, which left him in a coma until he passed away aged sixty-two. His daughter Mary, present at the death, reported the sad incident the following day.[25]

Just two years later, Mary's mother died in an horrific accident at her home on the Butts. A journalist from the *Coventry Standard*, reporting on the inquest, described the disturbing incident in detail:

> At the Summerland Tavern, Butts,[26] on Monday evening last, Mr Coroner Dewes held an inquest touching the death of Mary Taylor, widow, aged sixty-seven years. From the evidence it appeared that deceased lived alone. At about one o'clock on Sunday morning last [21 October 1877], Mrs Mary Waterfall (daughter of the deceased) was called to deceased's house in the Butts, and found her mother lying on the floor of the kitchen unconscious. Deceased expired about ten minutes after witness arrived.
>
> PS Gregory said that at ten minutes past 12 o'clock on Saturday night, in company with PS Wyatt, he was passing deceased's house. Four or five people stood near the house. One of them said, "There's a woman in that house groaning very much." Witness listened, and heard groaning. He knocked loudly at the door, three times. Not getting a reply he went to the back of the house, and knocked there, but received no answer. A young man broke a pane of glass, opened the window of the back kitchen, and opened the back door.
>
> Witness went in and found the house full of smoke. He ran upstairs, and on the top stair fell over something, the smoke

24 Birth certificate of Ellen Emma Waterfall, registered by Mary Waterfall on 18 April 1873.

25 Death certificate of Joseph Taylor, which states he was in a coma for fifteen years before his death – surely a mistake for fifteen days.

26 First opened in 1837, the Summerland Tavern at 49 the Butts was renamed the Fob Watch in 1981, reverting to its original name in 1994. Later incarnations were the Butts Retreat and Hamptons. It closed in 2017.

Summerland Tavern, Butts,
where the inquest into Mary Taylor's death was held.
Courtesy www.historiccoventry.co.uk

being so dense he could not see what it was at the time. When he was on the floor he put his hand out to feel what it was, and then discovered that it was the deceased; and he also saw a smouldering fire about the size of a plate.

He then heard a faint groan, and called out that the woman was being burnt to death. He took hold of deceased by the arm, and the flesh came off into his hand. He could not lift deceased up, but he extinguished the fire. He then opened the front window of the house, and broke some panes at the back to let a current of air through the place.

When he could see he found deceased's legs hanging down the stairs, her body being on the floor of the bedroom. Her face was on the floor, and her dress was very much burnt. Deceased was quite insensible.

Witness left PS Wyatt in charge, and went immediately for a doctor, returning with Dr Iliffe.

PS Wyatt said that whilst PS Gregory went for a doctor he got assistance, and removed deceased downstairs. He then went upstairs to see if there was any more fire, and found the small benzonine lamp produced by Inspector Elms. The lamp was caught in something that was hanging down from the dressing table, probably a table cover. Deceased was lying near. Witness obtained assistance, and got deceased downstairs. She did not recover consciousness. Witness was of opinion that deceased, on going upstairs with the lamp in her hand, fell. Her left eye was bruised.

Inspector Elms produced a small benzonine hand lamp, which he had found in the house.

Dr Iliffe said he was called to the deceased on Sunday morning, and found her lying on the kitchen floor of her house, as described by the witnesses. She was unconscious. Both her arms and body were much burnt, and there was a severe contusion over the left eye. She was in a state of collapse, and expired at two o'clock, which was about an hour after witness arrived. Witness had put questions to deceased, but she was unable to answer them.

Witness examined the bedroom, and found the floor burnt, and the ashes of deceased's clothing, which had also been burnt. There was a dressing table close at hand, near the bedroom door. He was of opinion that deceased was attempting to put the lamp on to the dressing table, when she fell, striking her left eye against the corner of the dressing table, the lamp falling at the same time and setting the things on fire. Deceased died from shock to the system, resulting from the burns.

The Jury returned a verdict that deceased was accidentally burnt to death."[27]

To lose both parents in a short space of time would have hit Mary hard, especially how her mother had met her end – but worse was to come.

Early in 1880 the *Coventry Herald* carried the tragic news that on 17 February, at just six years old, daughter Ellen had died[28] three days earlier at the family's Howard Street home after suffering from croup for four days.[29]

27   *Coventry Standard*, 26 October 1877.
28   *Coventry Herald*, 20 February 1880.
29   Death certificate of Ellen Emma Waterfall. The sad occurrence was registered by Mary Waterfall the following day.

Trying desperately to find a way to cope with their loss, Mary and Robert turned their thoughts to relocating; in time, they settled on Stoke Park, a leafy, spacial residential estate to the east of the city which had been created twenty five years earlier.

*

The haven where the Waterfalls would build a home, only for it to become the scene of a gruesome tragedy, was for nearly two decades the location of Coventry's massively popular annual steeplechase meeting, on land which was formerly part of Gosford Green.

Early in 1833, before either Robert or Mary had been born, the *Coventry Herald* carried an advertisement on their front page for the first Stoke Races; a steeplechase meeting to be held on 5 March that year and comprising three races, the highlight being the Silver Cup race. All entrants had to be registered at the Half Moon on Bray's Lane the day before the event.[30]

Keeping their finger on the pulse of excitement no doubt palpable in the city, the *Herald* informed their readers that a stand was to be erected on the course, in order to protect onlookers from the elements. As to the racing itself and prizes on offer, the newspaper breathlessly reported:

> A short description of the Cup will perhaps not be unacceptable to our readers. It is from Messrs Hamlets, of London, very richly ornamented, and is inscribed 'Stoke Races, March 5, 1833.' It weighs with the cover between forty and fifty ounces, and is of considerable value.[31]

The meeting was a great success, with the *Coventry Herald* subsequently trumpeting, "We can scarcely ever remember so numerous and respectable an assemblage in this neighbourhood, or anything that has given such universal satisfaction."

Giving the winners of each race – with the Cup going to Mr Phillips and his entry Tabberet – the *Herald* concluded:

30 *Coventry Herald*, 15 February 1833.
31 *Coventry Herald*, 1 March 1833.

COVENTRY RACES, 1839,

WILL BE HELD ON

WEDNESDAY, the 13th of MARCH.

(Ages reckoned from the 1st of May.)

The Craven Trial Stakes

Of 10 sovs. each, with 50 added from the Fund, for two and three yrs. old; two yrs. old, 7st.; three, 8st. 7lb.; once round and a distance; mares and geldings allowed 3lb. No public money will be given unless three horses start.

Advertisement for the Coventry Races,
Coventry Standard, 8 February 1839

From the remarkable fineness of the day, a great part of the beauty and fashion of our City were induced to honour the Races by their presence, contributing thereby to the gaiety and brilliance of the scene; and we believe we may now congratulate our sporting and other friends, on the permanent establishment of Races for the City.[32]

The proprietors of the *Herald* were right to congratulate the organisers. Another meeting was soon announced for the following year,[33] and the second event attracted an estimated 10,000 interested parties, including the Earl of Craven and his family, who witnessed Pilgrim win the Cup in a thrilling finale to the day.[34]

Six months later the course was put to use for a head-to-head match between a grey mare owned by Mr Johnson, landlord of the Star Inn on Bayley Lane, and a bay belonging to Mr Sampson,

32   *Coventry Herald*, 8 March 1833.
33   *Coventry Herald*, 21 February 1834.
34   *Coventry Herald*, 7 March 1834.

described as "one of the Gypsy aristocracy." Mr Johnson's horse won the £5 bet, settled over best–of–three heats.[35]

With the size of the event growing each year, it was only a matter of time before Stoke lost its claim to the name; it was announced during the dinner following the 1834 meeting that from 1835 it would be known as the Coventry Races.[36]

Whatever the name, the gathering held at Stoke each March proved immensely popular. It should not be a surprise, therefore, that the criminal element were also attracted to the meeting – large crowds always present plenty of opportunity for the light-fingered.

Mr John Hammerton, a farmer of Fillongley, was no doubt enjoying a day out at the 1841 Races when he felt his purse being lifted; Alfred Corbett, seventeen, and William Barnett, nineteen, were soon apprehended. At their trial the court, after hearing that the purses contained four sovereigns and a quantity of silver – and, more importantly, the pair's list of previous convictions – both were sentenced to fifteen months' transportation.[37] Thankfully for the two young pickpockets, their sentence was commuted to eighteen months' hard labour. Their fellow prisoners at Coventry were not so lucky; they were taken to the Prison Hulks at Woolwich, and taken overseas to serve their sentences.[38]

With crowds growing year on year, a new 100ft grandstand was constructed in time for the 1846 meeting, ingeniously built in a number of parts which could be assembled using pegs for such

35 *Coventry Herald*, 12 September 1834.

36 *Coventry Herald*, 7 March 1834.

37 *Coventry Standard*, 26 March 1841. Corbett had served six months' for housebreaking in 1839. His young colleague, William Barnett, seems to have been a serial thief. In 1829, at the age of seven, he had been sentenced to four days' imprisonment and whipped; in 1833 a month and another whipping. The following year he served three months' for 'riot and assault'. He received a further six months' for theft in 1838. [England & Wales, Criminal Registers, 1791-1892.]

38 *Coventry Standard*, 23 April 1841. The two criminals failed to learn the error of their ways; William Barnett broke into a shop in 1847 and was imprisoned for another six months. By 1857 he had graduated to forgery, but after trying to pass off a counterfeit coin was tried and sentenced to another six months. Alfred Corbett assaulted an innocent bystander in 1849 in an attempt to rob him, receiving twelve months' for his trouble. [England & Wales, Criminal Registers, 1791-1892.]

an event.[39] Yet that year's meeting saw more reports of the sort of problems inevitable wherever large crowds met. A beggar named Mary Smith, not having experienced much luck at the Races, afterwards made her way to the Rainbow Inn on the Alleseley Road and helped herself to a handkerchief belonging to the landlord's daughter.[40] She was awarded two months' imprisonment with hard labour for her efforts.[41]

Two years later, in 1848, two men got into a fight on leaving the Races, close to the Binley tollgate. On the recommendation of the magistrates the two combatants – Messrs Gilbert and Butlin – settled out of court.[42]

The same stretch of road that same day saw a violent accident caused by the recklessness of Nathaniel Harper, who was also leaving the Races. Riding his horse at a furious rate, Harper rushed straight into the cart being driven in the opposite direction by baker William Payne, breaking its shaft and injuring the driver. Harper was adjudged the guilty party, unsurprisingly, and ordered to pay £9 damages.[43]

Leaving the same Races were two young men named Thomas Haynes and Joseph Garrett, who had got into a heated discussion at the meeting. They agreed to meet the following Sunday and fight each other to settle the debate. Police Constable Elmer intervened and arrested them for a breach of the peace, with Magistrate Perkins taking a lenient view of their actions and giving them a lecture on their improper conduct instead of a prison sentence, binding them over to keep the peace for twelve months.[44]

More happily, it was announced that the splendid grandstand used for the past three meetings was to be erected near St John's Church in the city, offering the public an unrivalled view of that year's Lady Godiva Procession, taking place on 26 June – so long as

39 *Coventry Herald*, 13 March 1846.
40 *Coventry Herald*, 20 March 1846.
41 *Coventry Standard*, 27 March 1846.
42 *Coventry Standard*, 17 March 1848.
43 *Coventry Herald*, 12 July 1850.
44 *Coventry Standard*, 17 March 1848.

they paid the small fee of 2s 6d per person for the privilege.[45]

The 1849 meeting took place, as usual, in March. Three races were run on Tuesday the 13th, including the prestigious Craven Stakes which opened the event, and four races on the following day. Once again a large crowd attended.[46] What they couldn't have known, as they placed their wagers and drank their beer, was that this would be the last meeting of the Coventry Races at Stoke. As such, the winner of the Craven Stakes at that final meeting – to be revealed later in this book – provided a chilling premonition of events to come.

In addition to needing more space to accommodate the large crowds, complaints about the sodden ground at Stoke saw the Committee look for a new home, and a new course was built at Radford, alongside the Nuneaton Branch railway line.[47] While it was feared that a protracted illness suffered by the Clerk of the organising committee, Mr Pettifor, would see the first event there restricted to just a single day, instead of the now usual two,[48] happily he recovered and the Coventry Races were held on 12 and 13 March 1850.[49]

The ground at Stoke lay empty, the crowds long gone.

*

In October the following year, advertisements appeared for

> seventy-nine lots of eligibly-situated building land, in the parish of Stoke, within a mile of the city of Coventry, near the Bull's Head Inn there, facing Stoke Green and the Turnpike Road to Binley, laid out in Lots from 127 to 634 square yards each... in which substantial and convenient roads are intended to be made by the proprietor.[50]

---

45 *Coventry Standard*, 23 June 1848.
46 *Birmingham Journal*, 17 March 1849.
47 *Coventry Herald*, 2 March 1850.
48 *Coventry Standard*, 11 January 1850.
49 *Coventry Standard*, 8 February 1850.
50 *Coventry Herald*, 3 October 1851.

It seems many of these were quickly taken up, for in January 1853 a meeting of the allottees of the Stoke Estate was held to appoint a committee who were to look into the expense of having streets and footpaths properly laid down.[51]

In 1856 the Committee of what was now called the Stoke Park Estate Company placed a one-off appeal for iron founders to submit designs and estimates for a one-and-a-half mile long wrought iron fence, to include seventy-two gates. Tenders were to be submitted to Mr Henry Brown, Surveyor, of 12 High Street, Coventry.[52]

The development of the estate continued apace. The following year further lots were offered, at nearly half an acre each,[53] either for sale or to be let. Once again, Henry Brown was the contact for interested parties.[54]

But the semi-rural nature of the area brought problems as the 1860s dawned. An inquest into the suspicious deaths of Thomas and Adelaide Boothroyd, seventeen and fourteen years old respectively, heard that the siblings, from Ipswich, had died after eating poisoning fungi which they had picked in Stoke Park, believing them to be mushrooms. The jury returned a verdict to that effect, and appended a comment that mushrooms were to be avoided, on the grounds that it was almost impossible to tell which were poisonous and which were not.[55]

Two months later, three men appeared before magistrates charged with releasing a total of nine sheep belonging to them from a pound constructed on an allotment belonging to Henry Brown – the gentleman who had offered the plots back in 1857 – on Stoke Park, described in the newspaper report as 'Stoke Park Building Estate'. The animals had been grazing on the estate's common, but thanks

---

51 *Coventry Herald*, 28 January 1853.
52 *Coventry Standard*, 31 October 1856. Given the estate is now surrounded on three sides by a brick–built wall, it seems the cost implication of an iron fence was prohibitive. A document by Stoke Park Residents' Group says the wall was built c1874.
53 *Coventry Standard*, 20 March 1857.
54 *Coventry Herald*, 20 March 1857.
55 *Coventry Herald*, 29 September 1860.

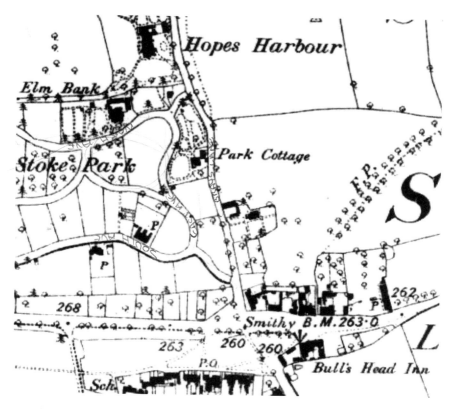

Map of Stoke Park c1883.

to the gates being left open had wandered off and were found roaming around Stoke Park. They had subsequently been locked up in Mr Brown's allotment pound. The owners, Messrs Woodward, Kimberley and Middleton, on finding their livestock fenced in, were erroneously given permission to release them by one of Mr Brown's workers, and they lifted the gate. When the magistrates heard from PC Brain that the estate gates were habitually left open, they had no choice but to acquit the defendants.[56]

Further allotments on the Park were advertised in June 1862,[57] and more work for Constable Brain came in 1864, when he was on duty nearby at three o'clock one August morning and happened

56   *Coventry Standard*, 24 November 1860.
57   *Coventry Herald*, 27 June 1862.

to see two men walking towards him, one carrying a large bundle under his arm.

No doubt thankful for something to do at that quiet hour, PC Brain surprised the man with the sack, while the other ran off. Inside were eleven rabbits and eight pegs used for pinning down nets. At the magistrates' court James Atkins was fined £2 with costs; the escapee, Henry Benson, was charged but claimed mistaken identity. A third man, Thomas Haynes, happened to be in the public gallery and was named by Atkins as the man who had been with him, not Benson.

After hearing all the evidence the magistrates threw out the evidence from Haynes, and found Benson guilty. He was fined £5, despite continuing to protest his innocence.[58]

The threat of poaching hung in the air over Stoke Park once again the following year, when two young men named Walter Orton and Joseph Claridge were charged with trespassing on the property of Mr Charles Sandiers, a wine merchant who owned land on the Stoke Park estate. When Claridge appeared before magistrates on 14 April 1865 he admitted trespass, but said he and Orton had not been in search of game. The kindly Mr Sandier said he did not seek a conviction, but had suffered so much damage to his land from trespassers that he wanted to make an example of this case to hopefully deter such conduct in the future. Claridge happily paid 10s 6d to cover the expenses, and was released.[59]

His companion, Walter Orton, did not respond to the summons and a warrant was out for his arrest.[60] When he was finally tracked down and taken before the magistrates, Orton claimed he had been away working in Leicester, and none of his friends had his address there. He, too, accepted payment of expenses to avoid receiving a custodial term.[61]

A letter from a green-fingered resident of Stoke from the mid

58 *Rugby Advertiser,* 10 September 1864.
59 *Coventry Standard,* 15 April 1865.
60 *Coventry Standard,* 22 April 1865.
61 *Coventry Standard,* 10 June 1865.

1860s revealed how the Stoke Park allotments were being put to use, when 'F.', writing in the *Gardeners' Chronicle*, happily crowed about a fine crop of grapes which had grown from vines which had been brought inside in May 1865 after failing when planted directly into the Stoke Park soil the previous September, with 'F.' writing "there was something wrong at the root."[62] Was this a case of the waterlogging seen during the Stoke Races?

Improved transport links saw the city spread out towards the east during the 1870s, and Stoke began to lose its independence. Part of the area would be transferred to the city of Coventry in 1899, and the rest in 1928.

But in 1877, familiar problems continued to surface.

PC George Caley was on duty in Binley Road in the early hours of 26 May that year when he saw Henry Benson, who had been involved in the 1864 poaching incident, walking towards him and carrying a bundle containing 'something'.

As Benson got closer and saw the officer approaching, he threw the bundle over a gate. Constable Caley asked, "Hallo, Benson, what have you got there?" Immediately, Benson reached into his pocket and took out the barrel of a gun, and warning "Stand back, you ———", struck the officer above the left eye; thankfully the blow was not as severe as it might have been, as PC Caley had been able to raise his arm and thus lessen the impact.

Sergeant Brain – promoted since his own tangle with Benson – was on duty nearby, standing in a field belonging to a local man named Clews when he saw his colleague and Benson come together. By the time he arrived blood was streaming down PC Caley's face. The officers managed to get Benson in handcuffs and went to retrieve the bundle thrown into the field, which belonged to a Mr Deeming. Peering inside, they saw two dead rabbits.

On searching the prisoner at the Police station PC Caley found a knife in one of his pockets. While the officer's eye and arm were

---

62   Letter reprinted in the *Coventry Standard* of 22 September 1865.

Binley Road, Stoke, Coventry.

painful for some time, it could have been so much worse.[63]

Four years later, another serious incident took place near Stoke. At ten o'clock on the night of 25 March 1881, engine driver Arthur Arnold was approaching Coventry in his goods train. As he passed under Binley Bridge he saw what he took to be a man lying on the embankment, six or seven yards from the bridge. Early the following morning, at around half-past five, he was travelling on the return journey when he saw that it was in fact a woman. She had moved forty or fifty yards from the spot Arnold had seen her the previous evening as he flashed past, in the direction of Rugby, but was now lying again on the embankment unconscious. Stopping the train, he and his colleagues took her aboard and on to Rugby for treatment. She seemed partly sensible, but incoherent.[64]

As she spent a fortnight recovering at the Rugby Infirmary,[65] the

63 *Kenilworth Advertiser*, 9 June 1877. Henry Benson was found Guilty of assaulting a police officer at his trial in July 1877 and sentenced to two years' hard labour [*Coventry Times*, 11 July 1877]. He returned to his wife and family, and resumed his 'day job' as a ribbon weaver, [1881 Census], but died in March 1882 aged fifty-nine [England & Wales, Civil Registration Death Index, 1837–1915].

64 *Nuneaton Advertiser*, 21 May 1881.

65 Martha Booth is recorded as still being at the Infirmary in the 1881 Census, taken on 3 April that year.

young woman's story came out – and what a story it was.

Her name was Martha Booth, twenty–two years old, who lived with her widowed father at 8 North Street, Upper Stoke.[66]

Charles Booth was a London–born watch dial maker, who had married Louisa Edwards in 1845 and raised a family in the capital. Sadly both their eldest daughters, Louisa Jr and Charlotte, died in infancy, and following Martha's birth at Clerkenwell in 1859 the Booths relocated to Coventry, with Charles no doubt following the work of the watchmaking trade. More sadness was to follow, when wife Louisa died just a year later.[67]

Charles had raised Martha on his own, and he was no doubt proud when his daughter found work as a nursemaid in May 1880.

Her employer was Elizabeth Ashbourne, the elderly owner of Binley Grange Farm[68] on Willenhall Lane, with her twenty–five year old son Oliver acting as Farm Bailiff.

Oliver had been married to Emily for six years, and the couple already had three children: five year old Alice, two year old Ernest, and William, just past his first birthday,[69] for whom Martha was employed to care for in her role of a nursemaid. Instead, she turned her attentions to William's father – or rather, responded to his advances.

It wasn't long before she was pregnant, and out of a job. She left Binley Grange just after Christmas, 1880, and returned to her father's home. Three months later, with her condition starting to show, Martha had no option but to tell her father what had happened. Charles wrote to Oliver Ashbourne, who agreed to make a one-off payment of £10. He said he would go to the Booth house at eight o'clock on the evening of 25 March, and asked for a receipt for the money which was would also confirm he was discharged

66 Address from 1881 Census.
67 Census returns; Baptismal registers; Death records.
68 Elizabeth Ashbourne was sixty–five years old in 1880. She had taken over the running of Binley Grange Farm following the death of her husband Joseph in 1876. When Elizabeth died in 1890 she left her estate to elder sons John and Walter.
69 Banns of Marriage; Census returns; Baptism records.

from any responsibility for the child.

Charles waited; Ashbourne failed to appear. After another five minutes he left the house. Martha subsequently went out and met her former lover. The couple walked around the lanes for a while, talking, with Ashbourne anxious they would be not be seen, and finally arrived at the bridge which crossed the railway line on the Willenhall Lane. It was now close to nine o'clock.

Ashbourne lifted Martha up by the waist so that she was sitting on the iron railing of the bridge – it was a manoeuvre he had apparently undertaken several times in other locations such as a style or wall, so she was unafraid – when he suddenly took her by shoulders, and saying, "Now, go over," pushed her backwards off the bridge.

Later, at Oliver Ashbourne's trial, Coventry surveyor Mr E.J. Purnell reproduced a plan of the area, revealing that the ironwork on the bridge on which Martha had been placed was a foot wide, and the drop to the embankment an alarming thirty-two feet. Luckily the spot where she landed was grassed, twenty feet from the tracks, ensuring she would not be run over by a train, and it was here that she was spotted by train driver Arthur Arnold an hour later.[70]

It was a miracle that Martha and her unborn baby had not been seriously injured.

The following morning Charles Booth went to Binley Grange and asked Oliver Ashbourne why he had not come as arranged, and enquired whether he had seen his daughter, who had been missing since the previous evening. Ashbourne said he hadn't turned up as he couldn't get the money together; neither had he seen Martha. He continued to deny having seen her for a week, despite Charles asking him four or five times.

Just as Mr Booth was leaving, Superintendent Hannah and Sergeant Moore of the Coventry Police arrived. They had been informed of Martha's story from her bed at the Rugby Infirmary, and had gone to apprehend Oliver Ashbourne.[71]

On 17 May 1881, before Sir H.C. Lopes, the Court heard evidence

70 *Nuneaton Advertiser*, 21 May 1881.
71 Ibid.

The bridge from which Oliver Ashbourne pushed Martha Booth.

against the despicable Ashbourne on the charge of 'Having, at the parish of St Michael, Coventry, on the 25th of March, 1881, feloniously caused certain grievous bodily harm to one Martha Booth, with intent thereby to feloniously kill and murder the said Martha Booth.[72]

After a detailed and passionate plea from both prosecution and defence, the jury took four minutes to agree a verdict of Guilty.

Lord Justice Lopes addressed Ashbourne:

> You may think yourself most fortunate that this poor girl is alive. If she had died you would have been tried for your life, and I doubt very much whether I should not have left you at Warwick to be hanged. I cannot pass upon you anything but the most heavy sentence. The sentence of the Court is that you be kept in penal servitude for a period of twenty years.

Ashbourne, it was reported, "appeared astounded at the severity of the sentence,"[73] and was taken down to the Warwick cells to

72 UK, Calendar of Prisoners, 1868-1929.
73 *Nuneaton Advertiser*, 21 May 1881.

begin his sentence.[74]

Despite the attempt on her life, and the subsequent injuries sustained, Martha Booth recovered well and was transferred from the Rugby Hospital. She gave birth to a healthy baby boy at the Foleshill Workhouse on 10 September, with the *Nuneaton Advertiser* of 17 September helpfully telling its readers that the child arrived at quarter past eight in the evening. His name is not recorded, and there are no further mentions of him in subsequent reports of Martha's life. It seems likely that the child was taken into the care of the authorities.

Martha's time in the Foleshill Workhouse resulted in another beginning. While at the facility she met a young man, another inmate, and just four months after the birth of her son they married, on 11 January 1882.

With the attempt on her life resulting in Martha's name appearing in the newspaper far and wide, this next stage of her young life was reported with interest, including the following from a journalist of the *Nuneaton Advertiser*:

> On Wednesday morning last were celebrated the nuptials of Miss Martha Booth – the woman who was thrown from a railway carriage [*sic*] at Binley in April last, by Oliver Ashbourne, and for which he was sentenced to twenty years' penal servitude – and 'Charlie' Scanlan. The bridegroom is a somewhat noted character.
>
> The young woman was removed to the Foleshill Union Workhouse from the Rugby Infirmary after the committal of the crime. Whilst in the Workhouse a close intimacy sprang up between the parties, which ended in their marriage on Wednesday morning.
>
> The bridegroom was attired in corduroy trousers, light waistcoat, velvet coat, and a new billy-cock hat; whilst Miss Booth, who, we are informed, looked remarkably well, was also respectably dressed. Her bonnet was dressed with a plentiful supply of white ribbon, and in the front was set out to advantage a large red rose.
>
> The journey from the Union to the Registrar's Office (Mr A.H.

---

74   UK Calendar of Prisoners, 1868-1929.

Masser's) was accomplished on foot, and many, for curiosity's sake, left their homes to a take a 'last fond look', at least for some time, at the 'happy couple'.

On reaching the office a very large crowd had assembled, and the two were the subject of much curiosity and laughter. However, they eventually made their way into the Registrar's sanctum, and the aged ceremony, which made them man and wife, was gone through.

After this the couple adjourned to a public house, where they agreeably spent an hour or two with several of their acquaintances.

Charlie Scanlan is, we believe, a native of Ibstock, in Leicestershire, and it is understood that the couple intend making their way to that place. However up to Wednesday night, we are informed, they had only got as far as Bedworth, when they proceeded in the direction of Nuneaton.

We are informed that at every public house they came across a thriving trade was done. The young man, who is not wanting in confidence, thus address the company present, "This is the young 'oman what gave that mon twenty year for throwin' her over the railway bridge. She wul sing yu a song for a ha'penny." He then exhibits his hand minus two fingers, which he states were smashed in a coal-mine; and finishes up by going round the company with his hat for coppers.[75]

Another newspaper reported that the newlyweds had no money, leaving the superintendent and registrar no choice but to forgo their fee.[76]

This happy-go-lucky start to the marriage didn't last; the couple celebrated their first anniversary in court, with Martha summoning Charlie for attacking her on Christmas Day. Coventry Magistrates Tomson, Scampton and Green heard how the husband, employed as a boatman, had punched and kicked his wife in the face, and threatened to throw her overboard. Scanlan confessed the crime, and was fined £10.[77]

75 *Nuneaton Advertiser*, 21 January 1882.
76 *Western Daily Press*, 13 January 1882.
77 *Atherstone, Nuneaton and Warwickshire Times*, 13 January 1883.

Despite this incident, the couple observed their vows and remained together. Martha soon became pregnant, and nine months after the court appearance, on 6 September 1883, gave birth to a daughter, named Charlotte after her father. Tragically, the infant survived just a few weeks, being baptised at St Mark's, Coventry, but passing away the same day at the family home, 9 Leicester Street.[78] The poor child suffered three days of severe diarrhoea followed by twenty-four hours of convulsions before passing away just seven weeks old.[79]

More happily, another daughter – Harriett – was born in 1885, followed by son Charles in 1887. Ten years later, the family was completed with the probable surprise arrival of Lucy on 16 August 1897.[80]

Five years after this happy event, Oliver Ashbourne was released from prison. He had served just eleven of his twenty years, and had spent a year at London's Pentonville Prison and then the remainder at Chatham, Kent. It was from the latter that he had been discharged, on 19 August 1892.[81]

A reconciliation with wife Emily followed, with the family moving to Corley, north west of Coventry, and three years later Catherine was born, joining Alice, now nineteen, Ernest, sixteen, and fifteen year old William.[82]

*

78 Near Draper's Fields, Leicester Street was obliterated when the Coventry Ring Road was built in the 1960s.
79 Death certificate of Charlotte Scanlan.
80 Baptismal records.
81 UK, Registers of Habitual Criminals and Police Gazettes, 1834-1934.
82 Baptism record; Census returns. None of the Ashbourne children married. Alice died in 1903 aged twenty–seven; William in 1916 aged thirty-six; and Ernest in 1940 aged sixty. He left his estate to his only surviving relative, sister Catherine, who herself survived to August 1984, passing away at Nuneaton aged eighty–nine. Oliver Ashbourne died at Wall Hill Cottages at Corley on 1 May 1925, outliving two of his children. [Probate record, which records that effects of £935 17s 5d were left to widow Emily.]

In February 1883 the *Coventry Herald* carried an advertisement for the private sale of a number of properties around the city, including two on Stoke Green and a row of eleven houses in nearby Bull's Head Lane.

Another residence on offer was a newly-built cottage in Stoke Park, which was offered with nearly half an acre of gardens.[83]

This would prove the perfect retirement location for Robert and Mary Waterfall. A year after the death of their six year old daughter Ellen, in the 1881 Census the couple were recorded still at 58 Howard Street, with Robert listed as a bicycle warehouseman.

But twelve months later, in May 1882, the *Coventry Herald* carried a listing advertising the sale of a "well-established bicycle and tricycle manufacturing business, replete with every convenience for carrying on an extensive trade, and in admirable working order." The business, which enjoyed a turnover the previous year of £3,000 (£200,000 today), was on offer due to the owner's retirement.[84] Sadly, the address of the establishment was not given in the listing.

Was Robert the retiring owner? He and Mary were at this time both forty-six years old; perhaps they had taken the opportunity to cash in on Robert's hard work, and move to the leafy new estate at Stoke Park in an attempt to move on from the loss of Ellen.

At this time, there were very few houses already built on the estate. The first house on the site was Park Cottage, erected by a local builder named Alfred Mault for his own occupation. Hope's Harbour was built in 1879,[85] and Elm Bank around the same time.[86]

The new home of Robert and Mary Waterfall was named

---

83 *Coventry Herald*, 9 February 1883.
84 *Coventry Herald*, 12 May 1882.
85 'The City of Coventry: The Outlying Parts of Coventry, Stoke' in *A History of the County of Warwick: Volume 8, the City of Coventry and Borough of Warwick*, W.B. Stephens (Ed., 1969). Hopes Harbour was sold in 1907 and renamed Harefield, and from 1919-1947 was the Stoke Park Select School for Girls.
86 Elm Bank was home to Siegfried Bettmann, founder of the Triumph Motorcycle Company, for forty years. He was elected Mayor of Coventry in 1913. A Blue Plaque was installed on Elm Bank in 2015 to mark his occupation.

S-32.

Bray's Lane,

Bray's Lane, with the south-eastern entrance to Stoke Park
behind the two girls on the left, 1914
Courtesy David Fry/John Marshall

Hawthorn Cottage, Stoke Park.
The conservatory spanning the entire upper rear aspect can be seen
in this sketch from the *Midlands Daily Telegraph* of 15 January 1906.

Hawthorn Cottage. It was situated to south of the estate, with clear views across the Binley Road to Stoke Green. And, as Robert had also purchased the two plots of land in front of the cottage, the view would be unspoilt for many years to come.

In itself, Hawthorn Cottage seemed ordinary enough. A two-storey detached property, in plain red brick,[87] the front door opened onto a staircase leading to the upper floor. Downstairs were two sitting rooms, with a kitchen and pantry to the rear, both enjoying views of the lengthy back garden. Upstairs, at the front, were two bedrooms.[88]

But there was one peculiarity in the design of Hawthorn Cottage

87 *Midland Daily Telegraph*, 15 January 1906.
88 *Coventry Herald*, 28 July 1906.

which was anything but ordinary. The upper floor at the rear of the property had been converted into a giant greenhouse, with glass panelling stretching the entire width of the building. It was only accessible from the upper landing, and had been built to allow Robert Waterfall to indulge his other passion beside bicycles – growing tomatoes.[89] With few neighbouring properties, the greenhouse – and the fruit of Robert's labours – was visible to anyone walking along Bray's Lane immediately to the east of the estate, linking Binley Road to the south to Walsgrave Road in the north.

Yet as the Waterfalls settled into Stoke Park and began cultivating a garden surrounding the cottage, problems were being reported. In 1886 the council had their attention drawn to defective drainage on the estate; having not only to keep their noses clear of the noxious fug, it was reported that several cases of typhoid fever had occurred as a result, some of them fatal.[90]

While the council seemed surprised, the poor drainage of area had been hinted at for some time, first with the sodden state of the ground when the Coventry Races were held there, and then with the wistful *Gardeners' Chronicle* report of 1865 which lamented the poor crop of the previous year's vines due to "something wrong at the root".[91]

In addition to this, the estate was not well lit; a problem which would have a bearing on the events described later in this book, and not addressed until their aftermath.

In 1888 an incident occurred which later warranted inclusion in Rev T.A. Blyth's seminal *The History of Stoke* (1897):

> March 31. An earthquake took place at 2 o'clock in the morning of this day. The *Coventry Standard* stated that:
> 'At few places, if any, was the earthquake so severely felt as in this Parish (Stoke). At the house in Bray's Lane occupied by Mr Jackson, the inmates were terribly alarmed by the oscillation of the building; the rattling of the doors, windows, and furniture;

89   *Kenilworth Advertiser*, 20 January 1906.
90   *Coventry Herald*, 26 November 1886.
91   *Coventry Standard*, 22nd September 1865.

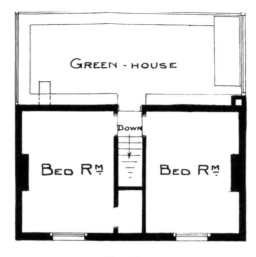

First floor

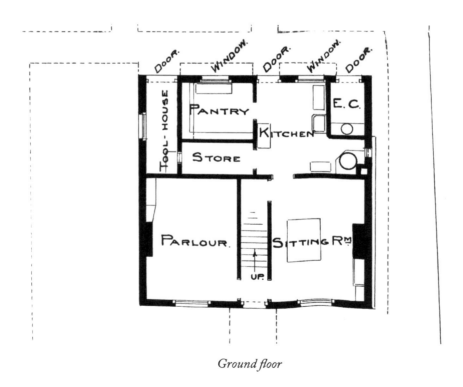

Ground floor

Floorplans of Hawthorn Cottage
drawn by architect T.F. Tickner for the inquest.

and the falling of a large quantity of mortar etc, upon the ceiling of one of the bedrooms.

At the house in Stoke Park, occupied by the Vicar, every ceiling, even in the new rooms and in an outdoor building, was cracked to a more of less considerable extent, the cracks extending in many cases right through the cornice. The Vicar, who had just left his study for his bedroom, states that the shaking resembled that produced by a large traction engine passing a house. The dwelling at one moment appeared likely to collapse.

The earthquake also much alarmed several persons on Stoke Green, at Stoke Knob, and in other parts of the parish. Some of the residents imagined that their house was being broken into by burglars. One man near the Ball Inn, on going downstairs, at the request of his wife, was glad to find that his house had not been entered, but could not make out what had been the matter.

It is more than likely that when rain comes it will reveal considerable damage done to some of the roofs.'

By 1891 Robert and Mary Waterfall were well established in Stoke, and were recorded on the census of that year alongside neighbours including carpenter Tom Woodward and his family, and Joseph Jackson, a paper cutter, and his own clan. Robert would no doubt have enjoyed a chat or two with a boarder of the Jacksons at that time, John Benbow, who earned a living as a bicycle machinist.[92]

Robert Waterfall himself was regularly seen whizzing around the area on his tricycle, but his time in the saddle was coming to an end. He passed away at the relatively young age of sixty-one on 15 January 1899, exhausted after a period of hemoptysis phthisis – tuberculosis resulting in coughing up blood.[93]

Following her mourning period, while Mary no doubt welcomed the inheritance of her husband's estate – worth £1,559 17s 2d[94] – she soon made it known that she had had enough of Robert's cycling obsession. Soon after his death she sold his tricycle, its

---

92   1891 Census.
93   Death certificate of Robert Seymour Waterfall, registered by widow Mary Waterfall on 16 January 1899.
94   Probate record, a value today or £125,000.

lamp and other related equipment to a scrap metal merchant for ten shillings, saying she was glad to see the back of it.[95]

Since that day, there had never been a bicycle nor lamp on the premises.

Robert's prize tomatoes were another casualty, as Mary lost interest in the conservatory's intended purpose. Instead, as one newspaper later commented,

> the conservatory had not apparently been used for some time, as it was minus plants of any description, but a considerable quantity of neatly-constructed bird cages were to be seen, indicating that there had been at some time or other a love of the feathered species.[96]

Like Mary's departed husband, those birds had now flown.

95   *Coventry Evening Telegraph*, 23 July 1906.
96   *Midland Daily Telegraph*, 15 January 1906.

MARY AND RICHARD

Mary Waterfall spent the next six years alone at Hawthorn Cottage.[97]

She was known by all to be of a lively disposition and very kind, keeping herself active.[98] But Mrs Frances Mortimer, who lived on Stoke Park at 'Glendene' with her husband Charles, a Coventry councillor, later said that Mary had told her she had been very lonely since Robert had died, and often sat up half the night reading in an effort to keep herself occupied.[99] She continued to attend West Orchard Congregational Church, where she had a seat in the gallery.[100]

Another neighbour, Mrs Eliza Woodward, lived at 26 Stoke Park. She was a sixty-one year old widow,[101] and had known Mary since she had moved to Hawthorn Cottage. The pair had become great friends over the years, and Mary confided that she didn't feel she could live through another winter on her own.[102]

She took to keeping a dog for company, but was forced to part with it when it developed a taste for chasing the neighbours' chickens.[103]

97   She is recorded in the 1901 Census as a widow at 18 Stoke Park – the name 'Hawthorn Cottage' not recorded – and as being of independent means. She was sixty-four years old.

98   *Kenilworth Advertiser*, 20 January 1906.

99   *Coventry Herald*, 20 January 1906. First names of Mr and Mrs Mortimer from 1901 Census.

100 *Coventry Evening Telegraph*, 16 January 1906.

101 1901 Census.

102 *Coventry Herald, 20 January* 1906.

103 *Coventry Evening Telegraph*, 27 January 1906.

Thankfully, Mary's loneliness was about to dissipate.

*

In 1901, Richard Phillips was living with his thirty-one year old daughter Mary Ann and her husband John Jackson at their home at 386 Stoney Stanton Road. Under the same roof was his grandson John Jr, just a year old.[104]

Richard had lived with the family since the death of his wife Ann four years earlier, on 8 June 1897, having suffered apoplexy for four days. She was just sixty-three years old. The death was registered by her son Walter William Phillips the following day.[105]

Until that devastating occurrence, the family had resided for many years in Red House Road, Foleshill.[106]

In 1901 Richard was seventy-one years old. He had been born to coal miner John Phillips and wife Mary at the small hamlet of Griff, and was baptised at the nearby village of Chilvers Coton on 20 December 1829.[107]

By 1841 Mary was a widow, John having passed away six years earlier. The census that year recorded the family at the home of her mother Mary Lenton. Richard, one of eleven children, was now eleven years old.

Ten years later the majority of the Phillips children were still with their mother at Griff, employed in the textile industry, and Richard was there, working as a ribbon weaver.[108]

This almost rural existence came to an end in 1857, when Richard married Ann Davenport at St Peter's, Coventry, on 13 July. He was now twenty-seven, earning a living as a watchmaker, living at Primrose Hill Street. His twenty-three year old bride was

---

104 1901 Census.
105 Death certificate of Ann Phillips, registered 9 June 1897.
106 They are recorded at Red House Road in both the 1881 and 1891 Census returns.
107 Baptismal record of Richard Phillips.
108 1851 Census.

a dressmaker, living a stone's throw away on Howard Street[109] – where Mary later lived for many years with her husband Robert Waterfall.

They soon welcomed a son, Walter, who was baptised at St Peter's on 9 December – five months after his parents' marriage – with the couple setting up home on Byron Street.[110]

Another son, William, arrived towards the end of 1860, and was baptised on 6 March 1861. His baptismal entry records the family now on Kings Fields, but this address would not last long either, as the Phillipses are recorded in the census of the following year at Turnpike Road, Foleshill.[111] Charles joined the growing family in 1862, being baptised on 30 December that year at St Peter's. Once again they had relocated – this time to Stoney Stanton Road.[112]

The family was growing, and Richard was becoming experienced in watch making. But as was so often the case in the Victorian era, tragedy was just around the corner.

Heartbreakingly, sons Walter and William both died on 10 November 1863 of that scourge of the Nineteenth century young, scarletina; Walter, aged six, and William, just four, died at their home on Red Lane. The brothers were buried together at Chilvers Coton two days later.[113]

The devastated Richard and Ann set about rebuilding their shattered lives. Another son, named Walter William in honour of the lost brothers, was born on 22 February 1865, being baptised at St Michael's on 6 June.[114]

Mary Ann, the first and only daughter born to the couple, arrived on 11 November 1867. She was more than six months old by the time she was baptised at St Michael's on 2 June 1868.[115]

Another son, Thomas Edward, was born on 17 September 1869.

109 Marriage record of Richard Phillips and Ann Davenport.
110 Baptismal record of Walter Phillips.
111 1861 Census.
112 Baptismal record of Charles Richard Phillips.
113 Death certificates of Walter and William Phillips; Burial register.
114 Baptismal record of Walter William Phillips.
115 Baptismal record of Mary Ann Phillips.

The family seemed to have put down roots at last; they had been, at this point, at Red Lane for over six years.[116]

But when Thomas died on 11 March 1871, not yet two years old, it was at Peel Street, Foleshill.[117] That year's census, recorded a few weeks later, recorded the family at that address, with Richard now forty-one, a watchmaker; Ann, thirty-seven, a dressmaker; Charles, nine, and Walter William, six, receiving an education, and three year old Mary Ann completing the family.[118]

Two final children were born to the couple – Thomas John on 12 December 1875,[119] and Wilfred on 3 February 1878.[120] Both boys were baptised on 24 September 1878, with the Phillipses recorded as being on Stoney Stanton Road.

They were, therefore, living very close to Mary and Robert Waterfall's home on Howard Street; it is possible that Mary met Richard at this time.

The Phillips family then moved to nearby Red House Road, spending almost two decades at that address before the sad death of Ann.[121] For at least forty years Richard worked as a watch maker, but for many years had then been employed at the Technical Institute on Earl Street, near to his home, cleaning the tools at the watchmaking department.[122]

On 24 September 1904 Richard Phillips and Mary Waterfall were married at the Coventry Register Office, with Mr and Mrs Percy Eld acting as their witnesses. The seventy-three year old groom was registered as living at 386 Stoney Stanton Road; the blushing bride, sixty-eight, resided at Stoke Park.[123]

Richard soon moved in with his wife at Hawthorn Cottage.

---

116 Baptismal record of Thomas Edward Phillips.
117 *Coventry Standard,* 17 March 1871.
118 1871 Census.
119 Baptismal record of Thomas John Phillips.
120 1939 Register.
121 1881 and 1891 Census returns.
122 *Coventry Evening Telegraph,* 16 January 1906. The newspaper reported that Richard visited the department on a weekly basis, and at the time of his death had done so in excess of thirteen years.
123 Marriage certificate of Richard Phillips and Mary Waterfall.

Richard and Mary Phillips.
*from the Herts & Cambs Reporter
& Royston Crow, 3 March 1906*

Mrs Woodward, their neighbour, later told reporters that the new Mrs Phillips had told her she had "never been happier in her life."[124] Given the tragedies she'd experienced in her past – losing her daughter, mother and father in a five-year spell, and then the death of her first husband, the tricycle-riding Robert Waterfall – nobody could begrudge Mary finding happiness at last.

*

Richard Phillips had not long joined Mary at Hawthorn Cottage when burglars took advantage of the absence of a neighbour, John Slaughter, who was away on holiday.

Mr Slaughter had locked up his home, Rushan House, on 8 August and set off on an extended vacation. He returned on 12 September – twelve days before the Phillipses' nuptials – to find the house had been broken into at the rear, and a great many items missing. Inspector William Imber and Sergeant Herbert Bassett of Coventry's City Police Detective Department arrived and created a long list of the stolen properly, which included almost a full wardrobe of clothing, enough crockery and utensils to stock a

124 *Coventry Herald*, 20 January 1906.

kitchen, and five bottles of champagne.

Two men, Herbert Stringer and Edward Haywood, both of Albert Street, were soon apprehended and confessed. Stringer, a machinist, told Sgt Bassett he regretted their actions, while Haywood, a painter, admitted they had committed the crime because "we wanted food."

Thanks to the efforts of the Police, nearly all the property was recovered.[125] Stringer was sentenced to five months' imprisonment, with Haywood receiving six months', having previous in the form of a fine for stealing two chickens in 1902.[126]

Having found love late in life, Richard and Mary Phillips were by all accounts devoted to each other. They were a hugely popular couple, often visiting friends and neighbours, with the compliment always returned. That summer they had a visit from Mary's cousin Robert Taylor and his wife Ellen,[127] and Mary bumped into Robert again on Stoke Green soon after, the cousins stopping to swap their news.[128]

In September 1905 Richard and Mary took a holiday in Blackpool.[129] While they were away, Hawthorn Cottage was looked after by Percy Eld, who also did the gardening. He had known Mary for sixteen years and was a weekly visitor with his wife, Phoebe.[130] The Elds were considered such close friends of Mary they had been their witnesses at the wedding.

Evidence of Percy's benevolent nature came that year when he and Phoebe adopted the infant daughter of her sister Jane, not long married to Henry Minten, a young German immigrant. Mary Magdalene Minten was a twin to brother Hubert, who remained with his parents, and perhaps the extra mouth to feed was too much

125 *Coleshill Chronicle*, 1 October 1904.
126 UK Calendar of Prisoners, 1868-1929.
127 Deposition of Percy William Eld in 'Criminal depositions and case papers: MURDER: Taylor' (The National Archives ASSI 13/36).
128 Inquest testimony of Robert Taylor in 'Criminal depositions and case papers: MURDER: Taylor' (The National Archives ASSI 13/36).
129 *Coventry Herald*, 20 January 1906.
130 *Midland Daily Telegraph*, 24 March 1906. Mrs Eld's first name from census returns. She and Percy William Eld were married on Christmas Day 1888. When Phoebe died in 1936, the following year Percy married Dorothy Morley. The groom was sixty-two, the bride thirty-seven.

for the Mintens.[131]

The Phillipses had barely settled back into life at Hawthorn Cottage when Richard's only daughter, Mary Ann, died on 28 November 1905 after a stroke which left her in a coma.[132] Since Richard had moved from their home to be with his new wife, she and husband John Jackson had welcomed two more children; Annie, in 1903, and Florence, early in 1905. The youngest was only eight months old when her mother died aged just thirty-seven.[133]

As the calendar ticked over to 1906, despite the cold start to the year the Phillipses remained active, and interested in local affairs.

Richard attended a talk from A.E.W. Mason, the Coventry Liberal candidate for the imminent General Election, at Stoke National School, across Stoke Green, on Thursday 4th January.[134]

A reporter admirably captured the scene:

> The meeting was a wonderfully enthusiastic one; "the atmosphere," as the candidate remarked, "was politically warm." The long, tunnel-like schoolroom was crowded well-nigh to suffocation, and the proceedings, which occupied nearly two hours – a number of excellent speeches being delivered – were throughout characterised by the utmost heartiness… Mr Mason, on entering, was received with a cheer, and when he left the audience responded vigorously to a cry of "Three cheers for Mr Mason."[135]

Richard took away a flyer advertising a meeting at Stoke for the following week, at which Mr Mason was to appear, and propped it

131 Marriage and Birth registers. Mary Minten was still living with Percy and Phoebe Eld at their home at King Richard Street when the 1911 Census was taken, now six years old. Henry and Jane Minten were living at an address on Swan Lane, with Hubert and their four additional children.

132 Death certificate of Mary Ann Jackson, registered 28 November 1905.

133 John Jackson Jr married Edith Lucas in 1926. He died in 1990. Annie died in 1965, unmarried. Florence married Leonard Hewitt in 1928, and died in 1986. Leonard passed away the following year. Mary Ann's husband, John Clarke Jackson, married Miriam Worrall in 1909, the couple welcoming daughter Phyllis the following year. [Birth, Marriage and Death registers.]

134 *Coventry Herald*, 20 January 1906.

135 *Coventry Evening Telegraph*, 5 January 1906.

up on the sitting room mantelpiece.[136] It was a gathering he would never attend; nor would he witness A.E.W. Mason winning the Coventry seat for the Liberal Party, enjoying a 10% swing from the Conservative MP of ten years, Charles Murray.[137]

Continuing with their busy social life, Richard and Mary planned a get-together at Hawthorn Cottage for the evening of Saturday, 13 January.[138]

There was a lot for the couple to look forward to.

*

The morning of Wednesday, 10 January 1906 started as any other. The calendar which stood upon the mantelpiece at Hawthorn Cottage was turned over to mark the new day, and at around half past ten Arthur Clews[139] arrived to deliver some milk. He ran Row Farm in Upper Stoke,[140] and had for some time supplied the Phillipses with their daily pint. As usual he went to the back door, where Mary took the bottle and accepted Arthur's loan of his newspaper, calling to her husband, who was in the sitting room, "Here, guv'nor, Mr Clews has brought you a paper." Richard answered in his usual cheery fashion, and Mr Clews went on his way.[141]

That afternoon, at a quarter to four, baker Daniel Shell[142] arrived to deliver bread. He had known the couple for ten months, and he

---

136 *Midland Daily Telegraph*, 13 January 1906.

137 Alfred Mason was a novelist most famous for *The Four Feathers*, published in 1902. He served just a single term as Member of Parliament for Coventry, retiring in 1910 to return to writing.

138 *Kenilworth Advertiser*, 20 January 1906.

139 Arthur Clews, fifty-six at the time of the murders, married Sarah Ann Hickman in April 1874 and the couple had four children. He died in 1936 aged eighty-seven.

140 *Coventry Evening Telegraph*, 14 September 1894. Address in census returns given as 3 Stoke Row.

141 Deposition of Arthur Clews in 'Criminal depositions and case papers: MURDER: Taylor' (The National Archives ASSI 13/36).

142 Daniel Shell, thirty-two, was employed by baker Mr West of Cross Cheaping and living at 6 Mowbray Street. He married Ellen Magson in 1903, but she sadly died just months after the murder of Mary and Richard Phillips, aged just twenty-five. Daniel Shell married again, to Gertrude Bell in 1919. He died in September 1962, aged eighty-eight.

The rear of Hawthorn Cottage, showing the kitchen door, far left, and pantry window. The door on the right was for the tool house. *from the Midlands Daily Telegraph of 15 January 1906.*

too went to the back door, where Mary took one loaf and asked him not to come on the Thursday, but to return on Friday.[143]

It was just a normal day in the lives of the Phillipses. At half past six that evening they were out for their usual stroll, and were seen by William Wright,[144] a cycle polisher on his way home from work. Wright rented a piece of garden from Mary, and had known her for some years. As they met on the Binley Road, opposite Binley Terrace, Mary cheerfully wished him "Goodnight," and they carried on their way.[145]

Just over an hour later Sarah Gadsby, a live-in companion to Sarah Ann Mason who lived with her husband Arthur[146] at 'Alton', diagonally facing the front aspect of Hawthorn Cottage, went out to go to the post office in Bull's Head Lane.[147] As she passed the Phillipses' home she glanced at their sitting room window, and as the Venetian blinds were open she was able to see into the room. On her return ten minutes later she glanced once again into the room, and saw Mary and Richard sitting together quite contentedly. She saw no light in any other room in the house.[148]

Mrs Rose Tickner,[149] who lived at Stoke Green on the other

143 Deposition of Daniel Shell in 'Criminal depositions and case papers: MURDER: Taylor' (The National Archives ASSI 13/36).

144 Thirty-five years old in 1906, William Wright had married Annie Morriss on Christmas Day 1896, having four children. He died in 1924.

145 Deposition of William Henry Wright in 'Criminal depositions and case papers: MURDER: Taylor' (The National Archives ASSI 13/36).

146 Forenames of Mr and Mrs Mason from Ancestry records. Sarah Jane Mason was forty-five years old at the time of the murders, indicating that her need for a companion was perhaps due to her husband's work keeping him away from home than an age-related infirmity.

147 The 1901 and 1911 Census returns list the Post Office at 32 Bull's Head Lane, towards the end of the road and near the New Inn. It was owned by Alfred Ward, a lithographic printer, with the post office counter run by his daughters Rebecca in 1901 and then Mary in 1911.

148 Deposition of Sarah Gadsby in 'Criminal depositions and case papers: MURDER: Taylor' (The National Archives ASSI 13/36).

149 Rose Elizabeth Tickner was married to architect Thomas Tickner, the couple having three children. She died just eighteen months after the Stoke murders, aged forty. Thomas Tickner went on to design the ninety-foot Coventry War Memorial; his winning submission was chosen from fifteen designs after his death, and the memorial was completed three years later. [*Coventry Evening Telegraph*, 17 May 1924.]

The former Post Office on Bull's Head Lane
(far left of the red-brick terrace, with white door).

side of the Binley Road, had spent the evening at St Michael's Parish Schools on Much Park Street with her husband Thomas. As they alighted a tram by Stoke Green, at around quarter past ten, she looked up and noticed that the lights were on in both the Phillipses' sitting room and bedroom above, but saw no sign of the old couple.[150]

A few minutes later Sarah Gadsby went to bed. As she drew the curtains to her bedroom window, which faced Hawthorn Cottage, she noticed that the sitting room blinds were still open, the lamp still lit, but there was no sign of Mary or Richard. Miss Gadsby knew it was their habit to retire between ten o'clock and half-past, and as if by way of confirmation she saw that the blinds to their bedroom window were closed.

150 Deposition of Rose Elizabeth Tickner in 'Criminal depositions and case papers: MURDER: Taylor' (The National Archives ASSI 13/36).

FOOTPATH TO
WALSGRAVE ROAD

JABETT'S ASH

BINLEY ROAD

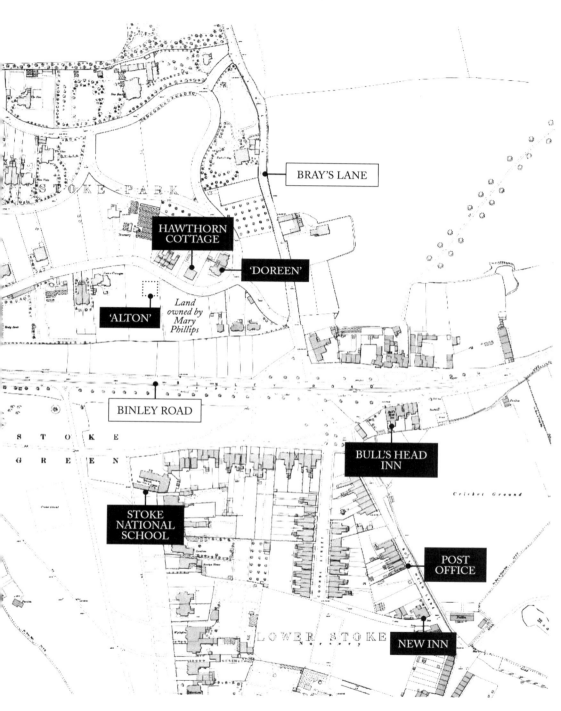

Map of Stoke Park and environs, 1903

It was a clear night, lit by bright moonlight.[151]

Living at the quaintly-named house 'Doreen', twenty yards from Hawthorn Cottage, were William Cotton and his wife Mary Jane.[152] That evening, between half-past nine and ten o'clock, they happened to be standing at their back door, which afforded a clear view of the rear of Hawthorn Cottage, when they saw beams of light intermittently cut through the darkness of the Phillipses' upstairs conservatory.

Mrs Cotton would later say that it gave the impression of someone walking around in the dark, wielding a flashlight.[153]

151 Deposition of Sarah Gadsby in 'Criminal depositions and case papers: MURDER: Taylor' (The National Archives ASSI 13/36).
152 William Lindo Cotton was born on 31 July 1875 at Chipping Norton, Oxfordshire. He married Mary Jane Simpkins (b1870) in 1902. Mary Jane appears to have died at some point over the next nine years, for William married Mary Burton on 22 July 1911 and the latter couple had two sons.
153 *Kenilworth Advertiser*, 7 April 1906.

3.

BLOOD ON THE CEILING

The following morning Arthur Clews once again arrived at Hawthorn Cottage around half past ten to deliver some milk. This time the back door was closed, and neither Mary or Richard were anywhere to be seen. Arthur noticed that the pantry window was open, with one sash pushed up, and some plates were lying in the flower bed underneath. On the other side of the path were some more plates, with two oranges lying in the grass nearby. Arthur looked through the pantry window and saw a pork chop lying on a stone slab nearby, but nothing appeared to be out of place. He left without leaving any milk.

He came again at the same time on the Friday – 12 January – and found the window still open, with the crockery and fruit still lying on the ground. When things were exactly the same on the Saturday, he came to the conclusion that the old couple had gone away for a few days.[154]

Daniel Shell arrived in the afternoon of the Friday to deliver his bread as requested by Mary, and found the situation exactly the same as Arthur Clews. He too saw the plates on the ground, and assumed they'd blown off the pantry windowsill. A mesh screen which was usually placed across the window was lying on the floor inside the pantry.[155]

---

154 Deposition of Arthur Clews in 'Criminal depositions and case papers: MURDER: Taylor' (The National Archives ASSI 13/36).
155 Deposition of Daniel Shell in 'Criminal depositions and case papers: MURDER: Taylor' (The National Archives ASSI 13/36).

A dog kennel sat close to the pantry window, its resident long gone; it was a reminder of the canine companion Mrs Phillips had once kept.[156]

It was only on the afternoon of Saturday 13 January that Mr Shell, arriving once again at the back of Hawthorn Cottage and finding plates, oranges and screen still in the same position, began to think something was amiss.

He walked round to the front of the house and across the road to 'Alton', the home of Arthur Mason, who was another of his customers. Sarah Gadsby opened the door, and Shell voiced his concerns. Mr Mason's nephew Charles Chouler[157] was visiting, and agreed to go to the Phillipses' house with Shell to investigate.

The men climbed in through the pantry window, finding no disorder in that room apart from the screen lying on the floor, and nothing amiss in the kitchen.[158]

As they made their way through to the front of the house, through the kitchen and sitting room, the comfortable interior of the cottage was revealed.

The ceiling, as well as the walls, were papered in the quaint style adopted in houses built many years earlier, whereby differing sizes of wallpaper were pasted everywhere, in the case of Hawthorn Cottage alongside a different wallpaper of a floral design.

On the walls were a number of sampler needlepoint canvasses, some pictorial – including one giving a representation of Adam and

156 *Coventry Herald*, 20 January 1906.
157 A draughtsman with Alfred Herbert Ltd, the name of this witness is consistently misreported as 'Chowler' by newspaper reporters – an understandable mistake given they were writing down an audible pronunciation. He was actually Charles Arthur Chouler, born in Burton-Upon-Trent, Staffordshire, in 1884. He was therefore twenty-two at the time of the Stoke Park murders. He was the son of Charles Chouler Sr and Elizabeth Sidwell, whose sister Sarah Ann married Arthur Mason in 1893. Chouler Jr married Olive Barnett in August 1908. Following a career in engineering, by 1939 he was working in Yorkshire as a planning engineer in the aircraft industry. Charles Chouler died at Leeds in February 1965. [Birth, Marriage and Death Registers; 1939 Register; ASSI 13/36.]
158 Deposition of Daniel Shell in 'Criminal depositions and case papers: MURDER: Taylor' (The National Archives ASSI 13/36).

Eve under the apple tree – while two handstitched poems revealed that neither Mary or Richard had forgotten their departed spouses:

At the dawn of the day
Came Mary away
To the sepulchre and tomb;
But how did she fear
An angel to hear
Say 'Mary, the Master has gone.'

Surprised at the sound
In silence profound
While trembling she stood at the stone,
When none did she find
To comfort her mind,
Poor Mary, the Master is gone.

Another nearby read:

When this you see
Remember me.
Though many miles
We distant be.

Performed by Ann Davenport
in the year 1866.[159]

Alongside these heartwarming works were a number of photographs, including two of the old couple.[160]

Shell and Chouler climbed the stairs, and looked through the door of the right-hand bedroom, which was wide open.[161] What greeted them was later reported as follows in the *Kenilworth Advertiser*:

159 *Midland Daily Telegraph*, 15 January 1906.
160 *Coventry Herald*, 20 January 1906. When sketches of the murdered couple appeared in the *Midland Daily Telegraph* of 15 January 1906, they were captioned as being from a "Photo by Jackson and Son'; this was Herbert Jackson of Ford Street [*Coventry Herald*, 2 February 1900; *Coventry Evening Telegraph*, 24 September 1905.]
161 Deposition of Daniel Shell in 'Criminal depositions and case papers: MURDER: Taylor' (The National Archives ASSI 13/36).

Richard and Mary Phillips,
'from a photo by Jackson and Son'.
from the Midlands Daily Telegraph, 15 January 1906

A ghastly spectacle met their gaze. At the foot of the bed, suspended from the bedrail by her nightdress, was the corpse of Mrs Phillips. Her head had been terribly injured, the skull having been battered in, and the face disfigured almost beyond recognition. On the floor, with his head under the bedstead, lay Mr Phillips, and the horrified men found that he too had been most brutally done to death. The upper portion of his head was shapeless, having evidently been beaten most ferociously by some heavy, blunt instrument.

It was apparent that both had been altogether at the mercy of their assailant or assailants, and both had been dead for some days. Both were in their nightclothes, and the woman had been gagged by a petticoat being twisted round her head, drawn tightly over the mouth and fastened at the back of the head.

The appearance of the room bore evidence to the terrible nature of the struggle which had taken place, and the ferocity with which the blows causing death were struck. Almost everything was bespattered with blood – the floor, the walls, the pictures, even the ceiling, and near the bodies were large pools of blood.[162]

162 *Kenilworth Advertiser*, 20 January 1906.

Shocked to the core, the men left the house by the front door. They had been in the Phillipses' bedroom for just three or four minutes,[163] but the grisly spectacle no stayed with them for the rest of their lives.

Unbelievably, Daniel Shell returned to his work while Charles Chouler went to the Police Station,[164] returning to Stoke Park with Detective Inspector William Imber[165] and Detective Sergeant Herbert Bassett.[166]

Chouler remained at Hawthorn Cottage with the detectives for around twenty minutes then returned to 'Alton', leaving the officers to their work.[167]

As would be expected, Inspector Imber's deposition given later before the magistrates recorded the scene in great detail:

> On arriving at the cottage I went to the back. I found the bottom sash of the pantry window was thrown up. This window is a slide window. There is an upper and lower part and the sides level...

163 Deposition of Charles Arthur Chouler in 'Criminal depositions and case papers: MURDER: Taylor' (The National Archives ASSI 13/36).

164 Deposition of Daniel Shell in 'Criminal depositions and case papers: MURDER: Taylor' (The National Archives ASSI 13/36).

165 William Imber was born at Corfe, Somerset in 1867. He relocated to Coventry in 1887, joining the City Police that September and serving four years as a constable before transferring to the Detective Department in 1897. He was promoted First Class Inspector in 1900 and Chief Inspector in 1903, the rank he held at the time of the Stoke Park murders. Imber would become Superintendent in 1908 and Chief Constable in place of Christopher Charsley in 1919. He retired in 1926 and died the following year at Poole, Dorset. He married Hannah Blackshaw in 1892 and the couple had two children, William Jr and Edith. [*Coventry Herald*, 21 February 1919; 16 December 1927.]

166 Herbert Bassett (1874-1933) enjoyed a nine-year career on the railways before joining the Police, first as a fitter and then fireman. He joined the Coventry City Police in 1897, moving to the Detective Department two years later. He was promoted Detective Sergeant in 1905 and Detective Inspector following the investigation into the Stoke murders. He later served as Deputy Chief Constable and Superintendent, passing away in 1933. He married Edith Wall in 1899; their son Herbert Jr was born in 1903. [*Midland Daily Telegraph*, 31 May 1933.]

167 Deposition of Charles Arthur Chouler in 'Criminal depositions and case papers: MURDER: Taylor' (The National Archives ASSI 13/36).

BRUTAL MIDNIGHT MURDER NEAR COVENTRY.

Artist's impression of the discovery by Shell and Chouler.
from the Illustrated Police News of 20 January 1906.

Just outside the window in the garden opposite the window there were several plates, dishes & oranges. Inside the pantry window was a box which acted as a table. On the pantry floor there was a dish and plate broken, and a wire blind also on the floor.

I got through the party window, unlocked the back door which was locked & bolted on the inside. The back door goes out of the kitchen. I admitted the witness Chouler and Sergeant Bassett.

In the kitchen on a table near the door leading to the pantry I saw a bottle containing a little brandy, and a candle and candlestick. In the same room on the mangle I saw a cycle lamp.

Going into the sitting room I noticed the Venetian blind down, the bottom slats being straight to about halfway up the window. On the sitting room table was a bottle containing a little home-made wine, but no glasses. On the mantelpiece was a calendar which stood at January 10th 1906. In the fireplace was a cloth covered in human excrement, stuck together.

Passing through to the front door, on the floor opposite the letter box were two *Birmingham Daily Mail*s dated the 11th and 12th January. The *Birmingham Mail* for the 13th January was delivered whilst we were in the house…

On going upstairs into the bedroom on the right-hand side of the staircase I saw the body of a female – Mrs Phillips – suspended from the bottom bedpost by the right-hand corner of her nightdress, her right hand resting over the bottom of the bedstead. The body was in a stooping position, the head leaning forward and to the left. Shocking injuries had been inflicted on the head, and the woman was quite dead and stiff.

Subsequently, on moving the body I found she was gagged with a pair of drawers. The drawers were tied once round and over her mouth, tied on the left side, brought round again but not tied.

There was a quantity of blood on the carpet on the floor immediately in line with the woman's head, and the drawers round her neck were saturated with blood. There was also blood on the ceiling immediately over the body, and on the wallpaper on the side opposite the body. The blood here was in spots. A blunt instrument had been used to inflict the wounds on the woman's head, and as far as I could see there was no appearance of a struggle.

By passing round the bed to the right-hand side I saw the body of Mr Phillips, quite dead. The head and shoulders were under the bed, the legs extending towards the window. The bottom part of the body was naked, and had only an ordinary shirt on.

On subsequently removing the body I found that shocking injuries had been inflicted to the head and face, apparently with a blunt instrument. On the soles of the deceased man's feet was a quantity of blood, on the calves of his legs was blood and human excrement. On the floor near a night commode was a quantity of blood and human excrement.

On the wallpaper were spots of blood. The bedstead was a half-tester bedstead, and the bed curtain suspended on the right-hand side was saturated in blood for nearly three feet up. All the bedclothes were on the floor – the pillows and clothing were saturated in blood. There was also a large pool of blood dried near where the deceased man's head was lying.

The Venetian blind was down. The window was open slightly at the top sash, apparently for fresh air.

On the floor near the blood and excrement I saw a tooth and a fingernail, which was missing from the deceased man's right-hand little finger and the tooth was missing from the mouth. Near his clothes, which were on the floor, was a pocket knife. The clothing itself contained nothing.

In the deceased woman's dress skirt was a purse containing 4/– 3½d. The skirt was on a chain near the fireplace.

On a small fancy table was a lady's silver watch and a gold chain. The two drawers in the looking glass were drawn out about half-way. One was quite empty, and there was nothing of any value in the other. On the chest of drawers just inside the bedroom door was a cash box. It was open and the inside taken out and placed close to. It was quite empty. Under the cash box, which was covered by a small matt, was a jewel box containing jewellery. In a drawer in the chest of drawers I found two silver watches and paper deeds of property. Everything was in a very methodical manner in the drawers.

As regards the deceased man, from the smearing of the blood and excrement I think there was either a slight struggle or it was caused by the deceased man in his death struggles. On the window side of the bed there were spots off blood on the

Inspector William Imber.
(photographed as
Superintendent in 1926)
Coventry Evening Telegraph,
8 January 1926

Sgt Herbert Bassett.
(photographed as
Superintendent in 1932)
Coventry Evening Telegraph,
1 January 1932

wallpaper…

On going from the bedroom to the conservatory, which is on the same floor at the back of the house, I found a piece of paper between the door and the doorpost, placed there apparently to keep the door from shaking. As I opened the door the paper fell out. I went into the conservatory. In here subsequently was found in a linen bag containing £16 10s in gold.

In the other bedroom there was no furniture but a few small articles. The blind of this room was up. This bedroom is directly opposite the room in which the bodies were found…

Before the bodies were removed [to the mortuary] Dr Loudon and the Chief Constable arrived at the cottage. A sketch was made and photographs taken…

Sergeant Bassett was with me the whole of this time. I had dismissed the witness Chouler earlier.

I went again to the cottage on Sunday 14th January, the next day. With Sergeant Bassett and Detective Cox I examined the house and particularly the pantry window. I examined the pantry window carefully. The catch was in a very dirty and corroded condition, with dust & grease. It showed no mark of having been forced. It was a very weak temporary catch, and the only opinion I could form of it was that it was either broken before this date or it yielded to slight pressure. The catch proper was in an upward direction.

I carefully examined the woodwork on the window frame and the window, but there were no marks to show that any amount of force had been used to open the window.

On my first visit the front door and back door were locked and bolted on the inside. All the windows were closed except the front bedroom that I referred to and the pantry window.

On my visit on Sunday 14th January I took possession of the cycle lamp (now referred to as 'the Stoke Lamp'), & the jewel box & contents.

From Saturday January 13th and onwards the cottage was left in the hands of the Police day and night.[168]

Two Police ambulances kept at the Central Police Station were driven to Stoke Park, and shortly afterwards Richard and Mary Phillips left Hawthorn Cottage for the last time.

Later that night flash-night photographs were taken of the interior of their home by the Police, capturing the bloody scene for grim posterity.[169]

---

168 Deposition of Detective Inspector William Imber in 'Criminal depositions and case papers: MURDER: Taylor' (The National Archives ASSI 13/36).
169 *Coventry Herald*, 20 January 1906.

4.

INSPECTOR IMBER
INVESTIGATES

The following morning – Sunday, 14 January – the photographers were out again, this time capturing Hawthorn Cottage and its grounds from the outside.

It was not a moment too soon, for very quickly the morbidly curious descended on the cottage to see for themselves the scene of such unspeakable horrors. The *Coventry Herald* reported how "hundreds of people found their way to Stoke Park from the various ways the house can be approached."[170]

One can image the street sellers along the Binley Road doing a roaring trade.

On the Monday Inspector Imber went along to the mortuary with Dr John Loudon, Coventry City Police Surgeon, to examine the bodies of Richard and Mary Phillips in daylight.

The good doctor had been born in Coventry and educated at Edinburgh University before returning to his home city to start up a practice. He had worked his way up to become District Medical Officer under the Coventry Board of Guardians, but in 1886 had sought out a new challenge by going into partnership with Dr Gould at Leyton, in Essex. At a farewell dinner in his honour, Dr Charles Webb Iliffe, Vice Chairman of the Board of Guardians, paid an awkward compliment to the departing medical man, saying he had "never known [Dr Loudon] to make a single mistake with regard to the diagnosis or prognosis of any complaint," but more happily

170 *Coventry Herald*, 20 January 1906.

described him as having "a genial, kind-hearted disposition, and an urbanity of manner which did wonders in aiding the recovery of patients."[171]

Dr Loudon enjoyed a successful practice at Essex for eighteen months, before returning to Coventry at the beginning of 1895.[172]

He was appointed Police Surgeon in February 1899 at a salary of £50 a year, which was in addition to the income derived from his private practice.[173]

Since that date, Dr Loudon had been called out to assist the Coventry City Police whenever medical expertise was required on an accident, assault or unexplained death. He had also taken it upon himself to personally train the officers in basic First Aid, with the result that twenty-seven members of the force had been awarded a St John's Ambulance certificate to mark their successful examination.[174]

He was soon involved in a sad local case. In February 1902 PC Sexton was on his beat, which in part took him along the canal towpath near Stoke Heath Common, when he spotted a tin kettle sitting by some gorse. A lid was fastened on top.

On removing the lid Constable Sexton found the kettle filled with a part of a soiled apron, which he removed, only to discover the body of a newborn baby wrapped inside. He took it to the Workhouse Infirmary, where Drs Loudon and Soden examined the tiny corpse.

It was a male, apparently having been delivered full-term, well nourished and with no marks of violence or any injury. The doctors concluded that the boy had died from exposure. At the subsequent inquest Coroner Iliffe directed the jury to return a verdict of 'Found dead'.[175]

In November 1905, two months before his involvement in the

---

171 *Coventry Herald*, 9 April 1886.
172 *Midland Daily Telegraph*, 22 July 1896.
173 *Coventry Herald*, 3 February 1899.
174 *Midlands Daily Telegraph*, 8 November 1900.
175 *Coventry Herald*, 14 February 1902.

Exterior of the Mortuary Room at the London Road Cemetery,
marked by the three arched windows.

Stoke Park case, Loudon had had the unpleasant task of pronouncing life extinct following the discovery of the body of elderly widower Thomas Shakeshaft hanging from a hook in the ceiling at his home at 6 Court, 3 House, Spon Street.[176]

On 13 January 1906 Dr Loudon had arrived at Hawthorn Cottage between five and six o'clock following the discovery of the murders and, with Inspector Imber, went to the old couple's bedroom. After a brief examination of the grisly scene the bodies were removed and taken to the Mortuary Room at the London Road Cemetery,[177] where a thorough examination was made by the surgeon. His findings, reported in grisly detail at the magistrates' hearing, were harrowing.

While lying in the mortuary, the bodies were formally identified.

176 *Midlands Daily Telegraph*, 20 November 1905.
177 According to an information board at the London Road Cemetery, the Mortuary Room within the Carriageway Tunnel was built in 1871 in order to temporarily store bodies in order to prepare them for burial or determine the cause of death. The Mortuary Room and Tunnel was used as an air raid shelter during the Second World War.

Interior of the Mortuary Room, where the bodies
of Richard and Mary Phillips were held.

Richard Phillips' son Thomas confirmed that the dead man was his father. He had seen him last on the afternoon of Sunday, 7 January, at Hawthorn Cottage. Thomas stated that his father had then seemed his usual cheerful self.

Mary was identified by her closest living relative, cousin Robert Taylor. Although they were not especially close, and he had not seen her since their meeting the previous summer, Taylor confirmed that she had appeared well at that time.[178]

*

The early efforts of Inspector Imber appeared fruitless. Excitement was stirred when fingerprints were found on the brandy bottle in the Phillipses' kitchen and an image of these was sent to the Fingerprint Department at Scotland Yard, which had been set

178 Depositions of Thomas Phillips and Robert Taylor in 'Criminal depositions and case papers: MURDER: Taylor' (The National Archives ASSI 13/36).

London Road Cemetery, Coventry

up five years earlier.[179] Sadly for Imber, the results proved that the prints belonged to Richard Phillips. Another set of prints – this time on the cash box – could have proved more useful, but they were not clear enough to provide a usable image.

The *Coventry Herald* reported on a strange occurrence at the Coventry Police Station, when a man called and said he knew something about the murders, and had a suspicion on someone. While attempting to pass on his information the man fainted twice, and his manner aroused the suspicions of officers on duty. When they investigated his claims it was clear that the self-proclaimed informant was "temporarily unhinged"; Police Surgeon Dr Loudon

179 The first conviction in the United Kingdom through the use of fingerprint evidence came on 9 September 1902, when forty-two year old burglar Harry Jackson appeared at the Old Bailey accused of stealing silver cutlery and medals, along with other items including a set of billiard balls, from the Denmark Hill home of Charles Driscoll Tustin. A thumbprint found on a sash of the freshly-painted windows led to Jackson's arrest and conviction.

was called, with the result that the man was deemed unfit to look after himself and was sent to the Union Workhouse Infirmary.[180]

*

On Tuesday, 16 January the inquests into the deaths were opened by Coroner Charles Webb Iliffe at the Union Workhouse, but heard only the evidence of Thomas Phillips and Robert Taylor as to the identities of the victims. The hearing was then adjourned to 26 March to allow the Police time to continue their investigation.

That same afternoon, a small group gathered at Coventry's London Road Cemetery to witness the burial of little Mary Dalton,[181] just two years old,

Coroner Charles Webb Iliffe.
from Coventry Herald,
26 September 1914

the daughter of ribbon weaver John Dalton. She had died of heart failure at the Coventry Union Workhouse the day after the murders at Stoke Park.[182]

The following day, 17 January 1906, a much larger crowd at the same location braved the cold, wet conditions[183] to pay their respects as Mary and Richard Phillips were laid to rest.

That evening, one reporter conveyed the scene with great solemnity:

180 *Coventry Herald,* 20 January 1906.
181 Burial Register of the London Road Cemetery.
182 Death certificate of Mary Dalton, registered 17 January 1906.
183 Weather taken from 'Coventry Weather Observations' for the week 12 to 19 January, as reported in *Coventry Herald,* 20 January 1906.

THE COVENTRY TRAGEDY

FUNERAL OF THE VICTIMS

The funeral of Mr and Mrs Phillips, the victims of the brutal murder at Stoke Park, Coventry, last week, took place at Coventry Cemetery today. Admission to the cemetery was by ticket, and the ceremony was carried through with the utmost decorum. A large number of persons assembled outside the cemetery gates, but they were extremely orderly.

The bodies had been lying at the workhouse mortuary, and they were conveyed to the cemetery in two hearses, followed by five coaches containing the mourners. There were no flowers.

The Rev A. Wilkes conducted the service. The deceased persons were buried in separate graves. At the service in the chapel Rev A. Wilkes made reference to the tragedy, which he described as a great and terrible one such as seldom visited in the city. In the presence of the victims that day they were tempted, he said, to indulge in feelings of indignation and righteous anger against those who has committed the crime. No doubt the guilty person was suffering in his own mind and conscience. Whoever he might be, they could only leave him to the law, and pray that He who doeth all things well might have mercy upon the suffering soul of the sinner whose deed had caused so much sorrow in their hearts.[184]

Both Mary and Richard had been interred in coffins of polish oak,[185] but due to their differing religious beliefs were buried in separate parts of the cemetery. Neither resting place had a headstone, perhaps to deter the morbidly curious, instead having a simple urn placed as a marker to their memory. Alternatively, it might be that their families could not agree on the wording for the markers, given that both Mary and Richard had been married before.

The undertaker was her cousin, Robert Taylor.[186] The bereaved

---

184 *Birmingham Mail*, 17 January 1906.
185 *Birmingham Daily Gazette*, 18 January 1906.
186 Mary Phillips was buried in unconsecrated ground at Grave 8, Square 83; Richard in consecrated ground Grave 220, Square 125. [London Road Cemetery Burial Registers.] The serenity of the cemetery is well worth spending an hour or two in reflection.

Mary Phillips was laid to rest in this section of the London Road Cemetery.

man, who supplemented his carpentry business at 16 Spencer Street by acting as an undertaker, carried his sad work assisted by his son, twenty-one year old Charles Ernest Robert Taylor.

Known as 'Ernest' or 'Ernie' in the family,[187] the young man had followed his father into the carpentry trade. It seemed only natural that the Taylors would assist in preparing their relative for her final resting place.

*

To the public eye the Police, led by Detective Inspector Imber, had no leads in the early weeks of the investigation. One reporter put into words the thoughts of many:

> The mystery of the brutal murder of Mr and Mrs Richard Phillips at Hawthorn Cottage, Stoke Park, remains unpenetrated. It was hoped by now that the police would have been in a position to

187 All official documents and newspaper reports give his full name, ie Charles Ernest Robert Taylor, but he was obviously not called that in person. Statements given by his parents name him as 'Ernest', the appellation I have therefore used throughout.

lay their hands on the perpetrator of this foul deed, but up to the present they have not, apparently, been able to do so. The chief difficulty, of course, has arisen through the lapse of time between the night of the murder and the discovery of the tragedy.

Throughout the week the police have been conducting their investigations with unabated vigour, even to the extent of emptying two pits on the Stoke Road, with the object of ascertaining if perchance any weapon likely to have produced the fatal injuries had been thrown therein, but up to the time of writing, the search has proved fruitless.

I have heard the question asked by more than one person, what became of the sharp little dog that Mrs Phillips used to keep, and which had been missed for some time. The explanation is, I am told, that he had to be parted with because of his propensity to chase neighbours' fowls. The owner was extremely sorry to get rid of the animal, for he was a faithful companion, and a thoroughly reliable house-guard. The probability is that had he been at Hawthorn Cottage on the fateful night, no murder would have been committed.[188]

Finally, towards the end of the month Chief Constable Charsley[189] issued a notice to the press, in the hope that it would result in information being offered:

MURDER AND BURGLARY

During the night of the 10th or 11th inst. the dwelling house of Richard Phillips, Hawthorn Cottage, Stoke Park Coventry, was entered by someone unknown by means of a back window, the catch of which was forced. Mr and Mrs Phillips were found with their heads battered in, the woman being gagged. Both were dead. Robbery was the object, but at present it would appear that cash only has been taken. Amount unknown, probably a few pounds. From the appearance of the deceased and of the

---

188 *Coventry Evening Telegraph*, 27 January 1906.

189 Charles Christopher 'Chris' Charsley (1864-1945) joined Birmingham City Police in 1884. As an amateur, between 1886 and 1894 he made nearly a hundred appearances as goalkeeper for Small Heath (later Birmingham City FC). He played in goal for England once, against Ireland in February 1893. Charsley was appointed Chief Constable of Coventry City Police in 1899, and retired in 1919.

room the murderer or murderers must have been carried away with them unmistakable traces of the occurrence in the shape of blood-stained clothing.

A cycle lamp (an illustration of which is given) was found in the kitchen. This lamp, so far as can be ascertained, was not the property of the deceased, and was probably used by the murderer or murderers. It is of the following description, viz: Small common plated oil cycle lamp (having been very crudely black enamelled over), bottom slightly dented, green glass one side, red glass the other. The side lights of the lamp have been covered over inside with thick paper fixed on glass with a cement or glue that resists heat. Oil holder slides out on lifting red glass up and is slightly loose. On back of lamp, which fits to bracket, is the figure of a man with cross on front and holding a lamp extended, screw at left side to fit to bracket. Name of lamp is 'Mars', and is made by Albert Frank, German manufacturer. The wick of the lamp is similar to that supplied by ironmongers for paraffin lamps, and has a single black thread running through middle.

Similar lamp in author's collection.

The deceased man's clothing appears to have been rifled, and a watch is missing. Description: Gent's metal case, full-plate. English lever, size 14, crystal glass, sunk seconds, gold hands, plain case, believed star and garter on case, key-winder, 'Walter W. Phillips' engraved on works and on dial, number believed to be 51,881, gold balance, 1881 stamped on some parts of works or case, not of much value.

In respect to the lamp, please cause every enquiry to be made at second-hand dealers, cycle accessory stores, pawnbrokers, etc. and particularly japanning shops, as a japanner may have enamelled a lamp for a friend: with reference to the watch, at pawnbrokers, jewellers, etc: and communicate any information obtained to the Chief Constable.[190]

An exciting lead was almost immediately uncovered when Mr Norton, an ironmonger on Coventry's Jordan Well, told a reporter:

> On Wednesday night – the supposed night of the murders – a man came into my shop about seven o'clock and asked if I could put a cycle wick in his lamp. I said, "I cannot put a cycle wick in, as we have none in stock. We have some paraffin lamp wick, but that would not last long as it gets clogged up with cycle oil." "Oh, that will do," said the man; "it will last long enough for me, as I have not far to go." The wick was put into the oil holder, the lamp itself having remained on the cycle, which stood outside.
>
> After paying for the wick the man asked for a piece of string to tie a parcel on his cycle with. He was given what he asked for, and having tied on his parcel, a long narrow one, the lamp was lighted, and he rode away.

Asked if he could identify the man again, Mr Norton said he might if he could see him.[191]

The following week it was announced that a reward of £5 was being offered by Arthur Seymour, the solicitor acting on behalf of Mary Phillips' executors, for information that would lead to the detection of the killer. He, too, paid particular attention to the 'dark lantern' which had seemingly been left at the scene by the perpetrator.[192]

The subject of lighting was also on the minds of the murdered couple's neighbours, who complained to the town council that Stoke Park was the only inhabited area of Coventry without street lighting, despite applications for this being submitted in 1901,

---

190 *Coventry Evening Telegraph*, 22 January 1906. Walter W. Phillips was, of course, Richard's youngest son. Why he would have retained the watch rather than give it to Walter is a mystery.

191 *Kenilworth Advertiser*, 27 January 1906.

192 *Coventry Herald*, 3 February 1906.

1903 and 1905.[193]

Another concern the residents had was the lack of Police presence, writing to the Council:

> That a window of the house in which the catastrophe occurred should have been left open for three consecutive days and nights without the police taking the slightest notice of it is sufficient proof of the interests of the residents being neglected.

At a subsequent meeting the City Council defended itself with a grim determination, in the process trampling all over any sensitivity officialdom might have felt to the deaths of Mary and Richard Phillips:

> Before the annexation of Stoke [into the City of Coventry] there was one [Police]man stationed there, Sergeant Rawlins, who had the supervision of Upper Stoke and Stoke Park and a considerable portion of the area adjoining. Since the district was added to the city two men had been stationed there, and their area was limited to Stoke in the city, so that they had nearly treble the amount of police supervision which existed in Stoke prior to its annexation. PCs Smith and Maycock were the officers stationed there, and these were visited day and night by their superior officers. So that the statement that only one policeman was stationed there was a mistake; there were two. The distract was scattered, and a good deal of ground had to be covered, but if they had ten policemen in the district he [Ald. Webb Fowler] did not think it would have prevented these murders taking place.
>
> Another question was in regard to the window being insecure. This window was at the back of the house. As to looking after the interests of Stoke, he thought they would agree that they were looked after when he stated that from five thousand to six thousand reports were made to the Watch Committee as to inspection of houses. The police had no right on private property, and in some instances they had been requested to keep off. Independently of this, the police examined the fronts of houses, and if anything was suspicious as to the rear they made further investigations. It would be apparent that, if in addition

193 *Coventry Herald*, 3 February 1906.

to inspecting the fronts of houses, the police had to go to the rear of the houses, the force of 86 or 87 officers in the city would be absolutely inadequate, and they would want a police force of nearly 200. They were not under-policed. The average towns about the size of the city was one officer per thousand, so that in Coventry they were slightly above the average.

Unless the police had a special request they did not go round to the backs of houses. It was not the custom to do so in other places, nor did he think it necessary. No instructions were given to the police in Stoke which differed from those given for elsewhere.

He thought it probable that the murder was committed by someone who knew the surroundings of the old couple, and when once inside the police would be powerless.

This was an important matter, and he sympathised with the inhabitants of the Park, and if there was anything further he could add he should be pleased to do so.

The subject was not discussed further.[194]

It seemed the council believed that should a burglar break into your house, murder you in your bed and then neglect to close the window on their way out, it was of no concern to the Police.

And yet, such a break-in would eventually provide the vital breakthrough.

194 *Kenilworth Advertiser*, 20 January 1906.

5.

THE BICYCLE WORKSHOP

As the calendar clicked over to March, the contents of Mary and Richard's wills were made public on the third, revealing that he had left £355 to his two sons, Thomas and Wilfred, while Mary – who had inherited the large estate of first husband Robert Waterfall – left an estate worth £1,888 5s 8d.[195]

While the press and public sensed that the Police had made some headway, little did they know that the prime suspect was already in custody – albeit on a quite different charge, one of burglary.

The arrested man was Ernest Taylor – the son of Robert Taylor, Mary Phillips' cousin.

Ernest had born at 16 Spencer Street on 26 July 1884 to Robert and Ellen. From an early age he followed his father into the family trade, and by the age of sixteen was already working as a carpenter from the long-standing home on Spencer Street.[196]

He had been apprenticed to a Mr Duggins,[197] but the older man gave up business and the indentures were cancelled.[198] This was at the beginning of 1905. By the spring he had decided to set up in business for himself, and borrowed some money from his parents to

---

195 *Coventry Herald*, 3 March 1906. Values today of £150,000 (Mary) and £28,000 (Richard).

196 1901 Census.

197 Surely Oliver George Duggins, operating as a building contractor from Stoney Stanton Road, close to Spencer Street. Oliver Duggins is listed as a carpenter in various census returns and business directories, and was in his mid thirties at the time he would have apprenticed Ernest Taylor.

198 Inquest testimony of Thomas Eales in 'Criminal depositions and case papers: MURDER: Taylor' (The National Archives ASSI 13/36).

build a workshop with a storage shed at premises in Jenner Street – just across the Stoney Stanton Road from Spencer Street – which in total cost him around £50.[199]

The term 'workshop' conjures up an image of a professional set-up which Ernest Taylor's construction doesn't deserve; it was more of a lean-to, built of wood with a corrugated iron roof. Still, the twenty-two by twelve feet space afforded the young carpenter plenty of room to carry out his new business.[200]

It was built for him by William Lenton, a builder on Cox Street, who had known Taylor for several years. At first William was invited to join Ernest in the new venture, but he declined saying he didn't have the funds behind him to begin a new business. Instead, in April 1905 he helped with the construction of the Jenner Street workshop.[201]

From September, and for the next four months, a series of regular advertisements appeared in the *Midlands Daily Telegraph*. The first, published in the 9 September 1905 edition, ran as follows:

C.E.R. TAYLOR.
16, SPENCER STREET, AND
JENNER STREET.

———

BUILDER, SHOPFITTER, etc.

———

COMPLETE FUNERAL
FURNISHER.

———

ALL KINDS OF REPAIRS CARRIED OUT.

199 Inquest testimony of Robert Taylor in 'Criminal depositions and case papers: MURDER: Taylor' (The National Archives ASSI 13/36).
200 Deposition of surveyor Thomas Tickner in 'Criminal depositions and case papers: MURDER: Taylor' (The National Archives ASSI 13/36).
201 Deposition of William Lenton in 'Criminal depositions and case papers: MURDER: Taylor' (The National Archives ASSI 13/36). Born in 1883, William Lenton was the same age as Ernest Taylor so the two probably knew each other from childhood. Lenton worked from his home at 49&51 Cox Street.

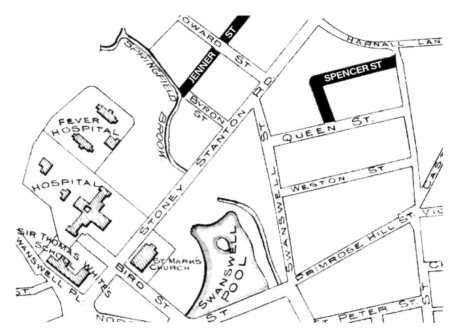

Insurance map showing Spencer Street, where the Taylors lived,
and Jenner Street, where Ernest set up a workshop

At first, business was good. Ernest carried out a good number of
jobs, and soon secured a contract with Mr Frank Betts,[202] a corn
merchant at 57 West Orchard.[203]

He had been courting a young lady – her name sadly never
recorded in newspaper reports or court records – and both Mr and
Mrs Taylor approved of the match. She visited the Taylors on most
Sundays.[204]

Life seemed to be going well for the young Ernie Taylor, who had

202 Deposition of Ellen Taylor in 'Criminal depositions and case papers:
MURDER: Taylor' (The National Archives ASSI 13/36). Born in
Coventry in 1857, Frank Rider Betts married Amelia Booth in 1880, the
couple having two children. Amelia died in 1895, and Frank married
Elizabeth Bagshaw two years later.

203 Inquest testimony of Thomas Eales in 'Criminal depositions and case
papers: MURDER: Taylor' (The National Archives ASSI 13/36). Address
from census returns.

204 Inquest testimony of Ellen Taylor in 'Criminal depositions and case
papers: MURDER: Taylor' (The National Archives ASSI 13/36).

just celebrated his twenty-first birthday.

But then, as is so often the way for the self-employed, business took a turn for the worse. Thankfully for him, Ernest was still living with his parents at 16 Spencer Street so his accommodation costs were low, just twelve shillings per week – but even those were in arrears. His mother would later tell the inquest that he hadn't paid anything since November 1905, when he offered ten shillings. Given his precarious financial position, he was not pressed for the rent money by his mother.[205]

Other debts mounted up. Ernest had not settled his bill with William Lenton for the work carried out on the Jenner Street workshop – some £3 19s 6d, a fair sum for a self-employed builder himself struggling to make ends meet. But, no doubt due to their long friendship, Lenton had not chased for the account to be settled.[206]

Another outstanding debt was the £2 13s 4d Taylor owed to timber merchant Arthur Newark for materials supplied back in May 1905, when he was first starting out. Despite approaching the carpenter for the money in December 1905, Newark had not received a single penny.[207]

That same month Ernest Taylor placed an order with John Caldicott,[208] a Coventry-based salesman working for the Gresham Publishing Company, for two books: *The Modern Carpenter, Joiner and Cabinet Maker* and *The Modern Cyclopedia*. The bill came to

---

205 Inquest testimony of Ellen Taylor in 'Criminal depositions and case papers: MURDER: Taylor' (The National Archives ASSI 13/36).

206 Deposition of William Lenton in 'Criminal depositions and case papers: MURDER: Taylor' (The National Archives ASSI 13/36).

207 Deposition of Arthur Peters Newark in 'Criminal depositions and case papers: MURDER: Taylor' (The National Archives ASSI 13/36). Arthur Peters Newark (1867-1940) was working with his brother George as a timber merchant operating from New Buildings at the time of his dealings with Ernest Taylor. They had inherited the long-established business from their father, George Sr, in 1895. As George Newark & Sons, the company operated until 2010.

208 John Underhill Caldicott (1842-1910) was sixty-four at the time of the murders, and had retired as the director of a magazine before taking sales orders for Gresham. He lived at 5 Craven Terrace, Coventry with his wife and daughter.

almost £6, to be paid in monthly instalments. The books were delivered to 16 Spencer Street as directed, but no payments were forthcoming.[209]

So, as 1906 started, Ernest Taylor had little money. He apparently had some work for a Mr Gorton on Bishop Street,[210] but little else.

Despite this, days earlier he had struck a deal with a man named Charles Furnival, who lived nearby on Stoney Stanton Road, for the purchase of some furniture, apparently in readiness for his forthcoming marriage. On 2 January Taylor had to go to Mr Furnival to admit that he couldn't afford to pay the £12 they had agreed. He left empty-handed.[211]

It was a surprise, therefore, when he announced on 4 January that he was engaged to be married to the young lady whose name shall ever remain unknown to us;[212] a fact he confirmed formally by writing it in his pocket book.[213]

How had Ernest Taylor suddenly come into enough money to persuade his sweetheart to marry him?

The explanation would not be long in forthcoming.

On the same afternoon, an elderly couple named Mr and Mrs Wilson[214] went to the Police station to report that their house had been broken into, and items stolen.

On the previous day, Wednesday the 3rd, the couple had gone

---

209 Deposition of John Underhill Caldicott in 'Criminal depositions and case papers: MURDER: Taylor' (The National Archives ASSI 13/36).

210 Inquest testimony of Ellen Taylor in 'Criminal depositions and case papers: MURDER: Taylor' (The National Archives ASSI 13/36).

211 Deposition of Charles Furnival in 'Criminal depositions and case papers: MURDER: Taylor' (The National Archives ASSI 13/36). Charles Furnival (1857-1939) was a Venetian blind maker living at 55 Stoney Stanton Road.

212 Inquest testimony of Ellen Taylor in 'Criminal depositions and case papers: MURDER: Taylor' (The National Archives ASSI 13/36).

213 Evidence by Detective Inspector William Imber, describing items found in Taylor's possession, as reported in the *Coventry Standard* of 10 April 1906.

214 Elizabeth Ball Dusson, born in 1834, married Joseph Vernon in 1876. She was forty-two, Joseph seventy-seven. She was widowed in August 1887, and on 1 October 1901 married widower Joseph Wilson, whose wife Sarah had died the previous December.

to bed at quarter past eight. Before retiring, they went round the house making sure all the doors were locked and windows fastened. Satisfied, they then went to bed.

Between three and four o'clock in the morning of the 4th Mrs Wilson was woken by a noise from downstairs. Waking her husband, the old couple strained their ears but heard no more, so went back to sleep and were undisturbed for the rest of the night.

The following morning Mrs Wilson went downstairs to find the doors downstairs open. She went back to the bedroom and told her husband, then both returned to investigate.

The kitchen windows and door were now wide open. A hole had been expertly cut in the door, seemingly using a carpenter's brace and drill bit, just large enough for a hand to reach through and open the door using the inside handle.

Wandering, dazed, into the sitting room, Mrs Wilson found things in complete disarray. A small box was lying discarded, its usual contents of a bead and gold snake bracelet, a metal chain and gold locket, and a cameo brooch all missing.

Another box had been left open, ten silver teaspoons and a plated salt spoon taken from therein. Also missing was a box of twenty-four farthings, a bottle of wine and, bizarrely, a crocheted toilet cover.

Detective Sergeant Bassett and Detective Cox soon arrived at the house, and found that the hole in the door had been repaired, and a bolt put onto the outer door. The work had been carried out that morning by Mrs Wilson's next door neighbour – Ernest Taylor. He was paid four shillings for his efforts[215] which, albeit welcome, were according to Mrs Wilson not to a very high standard.[216]

The Wilsons' home at 17 Spencer Street was separated at the back from the Taylors at No. 16 by a four-foot wall.[217]

Detectives Bassett and Cox took details and began their investigation.

*

215 *Kenilworth Advertiser*, 10 February 1906.
216 *Bristol Times and Mirror*, 10 December 1906.
217 *Kenilworth Advertiser*, 10 February 1906.

The Rose and Woodbine.

At 3.30pm that day - as Mr and Mrs Wilson were reciting the list of stolen items to detectives - Ernest Taylor entered the Rose and Woodbine at 78 Stoney Stanton Road[218] and ordered half a pint of beer. Quickly downing most of it, he popped outside for a few minutes then returned to finish off the ale, afterwards asking landlord John Evans for a half a quart of rum. Asked to pay for his drinks, Taylor dug deep into his pockets and brought out ten farthings and a halfpenny, which Mr Evans accepted.[219] He didn't know it, but the bill had just been settled by the Wilsons.

On 9 January another order was placed with publishing agent John Caldicott by Ernest Taylor, this time for a complete set of the works of Charles Dickens. They were delivered the following day,[220]

218 The Rose and Woodbine appeared in directories from 1850 onwards, with the present building being constructed in 1898. It closed in 2010. John Evans, who served Ernest Taylor his ale and rum, left in 1909.
219 *Kenilworth Advertiser*, 10 February 1906.
220 Deposition of John Underhill Caldicott in 'Criminal depositions and case papers: MURDER: Taylor' (The National Archives ASSI 13/36).

The Alma.

but the proposed reader, Ernest Taylor, was in no mood to make a start; he was, as we shall see, otherwise occupied. Not unreasonably, having not received a single payment for the orders Gresham later sent their man to collect the books.[221]

On that afternoon of 10 January – while Richard and Mary Phillips were at home chatting with baker's delivery man Daniel Shell and otherwise enjoying what would turn out to be their last day – Ernest Taylor walked into the Alma Inn on the corner of Stoney Stanton Road and Howard Street, and just around the corner from Jenner Street.[222] He was with another man, and called

221 Deposition of John Underhill Caldicott in 'Criminal depositions and case papers: MURDER: Taylor' (The National Archives ASSI 13/36).
222 The Alma Inn served customers before 1856, when it is first mentioned, and operated for more than a century before closing in the 1980s in order to make way for the expansion of the nearby hospital. Amos Statham (1882-1946) took over the licence of the Alma from his father Arthur in April 1904, and left in 1908 when William Collins took over as landlord. Amos was recorded in the 1911 Census as being landlord of the Prince of Wales, Leamington Spa.

for a couple of drinks.

After landlord Amos Statham had served them, the young customer tried to pay with ten farthings and a couple of halfpennies. Statham refused the farthings, so Taylor instead paid with a threepenny bit, two farthings and two halfpennies.

Although he seemed sober - but perhaps showing off to his drinking companion - Taylor flipped the tails of his coat to one side, exposing the top of a revolver. "I could get £2 or £3 on this article," he boasted to Mr Statham.

He then teased the landlord by saying, "You need not be jealous because I have been drinking at George Kaye's."[223]

A little later, Taylor got into an argument with another drinker and the landlord had had enough. He took hold of the young man and, with the help of another man in the bar named Walton, relieved Taylor of the revolver before putting him out on the street.

On examining the firearm Statham saw that it was loaded in five chambers, with the sixth empty.

Early the next morning – just a few hours after the murders in Stoke Park – Ernest Taylor arrived again at the door of the Alma. It was only 7.30am, and Mr Statham was not yet up. Returning half an hour later, he was allowed into the tavern. The landlord noticed that he looked "a bit slovenly", as though he had been at work rather than having just risen, and he seemed "a bit wild". What was the reason?

Taylor asked for his revolver to be returned, to which Statham replied that he had better see Mr Walton – who happened to be a retired Police inspector.[224]

223 *Kenilworth Advertiser*, 10 February 1906. This was the Gloucester Arms on the other side of Stoney Stanton Road, where George Kaye was landlord from 1903-1919. Kaye would later tell the inquest that while Taylor had been in his public house a few times in recent months, it was never for more than a couple of minutes and he had never offered any farthings as payment.

224 Surely George Walton of 60 Stoney Stanton Road, yards from the Alma. Born in 1858, George Walton joined Coventry City Police in April 1876. He became sergeant in 1883 and inspector in 1891. He was promoted chief inspector in 1894, before retiring in 1903. Walton died in 1914. [*Coventry Evening Telegraph*, 22 July 1914.]

Ernest left, and returned a couple of hours later after Walton himself had arrived at the pub. Asking again for the revolver, he was told he had to go to the Police station for it. Unknown to him, the firearm was still in Statham's possession. After Taylor had left the landlord gave it to Mr Walton, who later took it to his former colleagues.[225]

Retired Chief Inspector George Walton.
from Coventry Evening Telegraph,
22 July 1914

*

It took Ernest Taylor more than a week to visit the Police station. On Friday 19 January he arrived at the office of Inspector William Imber, telling the detective he had gone to see him about the confiscated revolver. Having carefully considered the fact that he had no licence, Taylor conceded he would rather pay the ten shilling licence fee than receive a summons.

Imber took the opportunity to ask where the young man had been on the nights of 3 and 10 January. Perhaps realising that the officer already had information which identified him as the burglar who had relieved the Wilsons of their cache of farthings and other items, Taylor ignored that date and instead replied:

> On the evening the 10th I was playing darts with the landlord of the Woolpack, Spon Street. From there I went to Jordan's, manager at Dresden's, Cross Cheaping, had supper and left about 11.20, got home at 11.35. Went to bed, got up next morning, had breakfast and went to the Alma Inn.[226]

225 Deposition of Amos Statham in 'Criminal depositions and case papers: MURDER: Taylor' (The National Archives ASSI 13/36).
226 Deposition of Inspector William Imber in 'Criminal depositions and case papers: MURDER: Taylor' (The National Archives ASSI 13/36).

This was a story which Imber could pay close attention to – and naturally, he did.

The landlord of the Woolpack on Spon Street,[227] William Hamson, said he had known Taylor for three or four years, and had given him odd carpentry jobs from time to time.

Ernest had indeed gone into the pub on the evening of 10 January, and Mr Hamson said that while in his opinion he was not drunk, there was *something* strange about his demeanour:

> He was playing darts. He seemed rather excited. I had never seen him like that before. He seemed wild and funny, and very much different to what I had ever seen him before. He was throwing darts about broadcast and not at the board... He was excited to start with and got worse.[228]

A man named William Scott was in the Woolpack at the same time, and confirmed that he had played darts with Taylor. His behaviour left Mr Scott with the impression that he was very drunk; Ernest was told to leave at around 10.15pm, having thrown two darts at the landlord's hat – which was on his head at the time.[229]

But Ernest Taylor had already been drinking earlier that day, long before he arrived at the Woolpack. Inspector Imber learned from Joseph Chantrill, foreman of Messrs Franks' Weaving Factory on West Orchard, that Ernest Taylor had been on the premises at around half-past six, clearly the worse for wear. Although he had carried out odd jobs at the factory in the past, he had no reason to be there that day.[230]

---

227 The Woolpack at 149 Spon Street is first mentioned in records in 1756. It closed on 31 May 1970 after more than two hundred years of serving pints.

228 Deposition of William Hambson in 'Criminal depositions and case papers: MURDER: Taylor' (The National Archives ASSI 13/36).

229 Deposition of William Scott in 'Criminal depositions and case papers: MURDER: Taylor' (The National Archives ASSI 13/36). Cycle polisher William Scott lived at 163 Spon Street with his wife Ruth and their family.

230 Deposition of Joseph Chantrill in 'Criminal depositions and case papers: MURDER: Taylor' (The National Archives ASSI 13/36). Joseph Chantrill (1858-1922) married Evelyn Riley in 1910. Their children were Marguerite and George.

One of the women employed at the factory, Elizabeth Bunney, revealed that Taylor was "rather forward" with her, and she could smell beer on his breath. After leaving work at seven o'clock, Elizabeth stopped on the corner of Well Street to chat briefly with her work colleagues, and there she saw Ernest Taylor again; he was turning into Well Street itself, in the direction of Spon Street and the Woolpack.[231]

Charles Jordan, manager at Dresden's tailors on Cross Cheaping, said he'd known Ernest Taylor for several months, since Easter 1905. When Taylor arrived at his accommodation at the back of the business, it was between 10.25 and 10.30pm. Mr Jordan felt that his friend was almost drunk. He stopped for supper with Charles and his wife, and left a few minutes before eleven, saying he was going to a club in either Much Park Street or Little Park Street, Mr Jordan couldn't recall.[232]

Next, Imber had to visit Taylor's parents at Spencer Street to get their story. What they told him greatly worsened matters for their son.

Mrs Taylor told the detective that on the night of 10 January she was not feeling well, so went to bed earlier than usual - around ten o'clock. Her husband came up around half an hour later. She did not see or hear Ernest come home.

The following morning, Ellen went downstairs just before seven and saw him standing in the living room, warming his hands on the fire. When asked why he had not gone home the previous night, Ernest said he'd "broken the pledge" and got drunk and, too embarrassed to go home and face his parents, had slept in the Jenner Street workshop. There was, indeed, a light coating of sawdust on

---

231 Deposition of Elizabeth Bunney in 'Criminal depositions and case papers: MURDER: Taylor' (The National Archives ASSI 13/36). Elizabeth Bunney was born at Eastern Green, Coventry in October 1881. Following her father Joseph's death in 1883, mother Hannah married Thomas Gilkes, who raised Elizabeth. She married Frank Cox in 1909 and the couple had two daughters, Evelyn and Frances. Elizabeth died in 1974 aged ninety-two.

232 Deposition of Charles Jordan in 'Criminal depositions and case papers: MURDER: Taylor' (The National Archives ASSI 13/36).

his coat. As a rule, said Mrs Taylor, he drank water with his dinner and milk at supper, so to her his excuse of avoiding her and her husband due to being drunk was entirely possible.

Imber showed her the bicycle lamp found at Hawthorn Cottage, and noted that she nearly fainted at the sight of it – whether through her illness or recognition was uncertain. Mrs Taylor admitted that her son had until recently owned a similar lamp, which had been kept on the shelf in the scullery. It was not there now.[233]

Robert Taylor agreed with his wife's version of events, adding that they had left a light burning until midnight when it was extinguished; Ernest had not returned home by that time.

The following morning Mr Taylor rose at 6.20am and lit the fire before heading to the kitchen and opening the door to the back yard, then washing himself at the sink. As he did so, he heard his son approach the house and walk through the back door, saying "Good morning" as he entered.

Having warmed himself in front of the fire, Ernest sat down to a good breakfast. Robert Taylor said that he had ample opportunity to observe his son before leaving for work at 7.45am, and swore there was no blood on any of his clothing.

But Robert, too, had been greatly affected by the sight of the Stoke Lamp. He would later tell the inquest:

> Inspector Imber lifted a lamp from the table and said "Have you seen this before?" I went faint. After I recovered he said, "Have you seen this lamp before?" I said, "I see the lamp, but I don't recognise the lamp as the one I saw at Hawthorn Cottage."

How did Robert Taylor see a lamp at Hawthorn Cottage? Is it simply a transcription error by the inquest clerk, or something more sinister?

Whatever the reason for the Taylors being so visibly affected by the lamp produced by Imber, the fact that Ernest Taylor had lied about going home after visiting the Jordans in itself cast him in a

---

233 Deposition of Ellen Taylor in 'Criminal depositions and case papers: MURDER: Taylor' (The National Archives ASSI 13/36).

very bad light.[234]

*

Finally, a breakthrough was made. On Sunday, 14 January, when news of the murders had broken, two men had visited Coventry Police station separately to report strange events which had occurred in the early hours of 11 January, when it was assumed the killings had taken place.

Machine driller Benjamin Taylor had worked a night shift at his employers, Alfred Herbert Ltd of the Butts, and clocked off at 4.00am. He walked to his home at 74 Bulls Head Lane,[235] and at around 4.20 to 4.30 he was on the Binley Road, walking with Stoke Green on his right and about to pass Stoke Park on his left, on the other side of the road. It was a clear night, with bright moonlight.

As he passed Jabett's Ash, on the opposite side of the road, he noticed two men walking towards him, on the Stoke Park side and twenty to thirty yards from the estate. Taylor had just enough time to note their appearance. One, who appeared to be younger, was about 5ft 7in or 5ft 8in tall, of an average build. He was dressed in dark clothing and sporting a dark hat of a Trilby style; he appeared to be around thirty years old. The other man, who Taylor saw in profile only, was older.

As they were almost parallel to him the men suddenly became aware of his presence, and turned and ran back in the direction from which they had come.

Stunned, Taylor stood rooted to the spot for a moment and then ran after the men. He was just in time to see one – the elder man – run into the entrance to Stoke Park, and the younger man go into a footpath immediately before the turn into the estate.[236]

234 Inquest testimony of Robert Taylor in 'Criminal depositions and case papers: MURDER: Taylor' (The National Archives ASSI 13/36).
235 Deposition of Benjamin Taylor in 'Criminal depositions and case papers: MURDER: Taylor' (The National Archives ASSI 13/36).
236 Ibid.

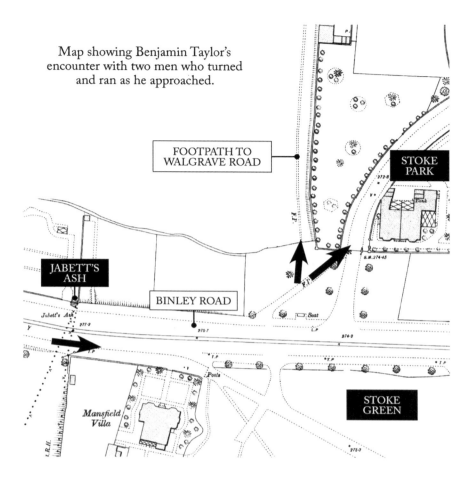

Map showing Benjamin Taylor's encounter with two men who turned and ran as he approached.

A few minutes later a haulier named John Boneham[237] was walking along the Walsgrave Road, north of Stoke Park, to visit his stables in a field which bordered the footpath running from the Walsgrave Road to Binley Road to the south. As he passed the Old Ball Inn at Stoke Knob he spotted a man walking towards him, on the same side of the street. He had not been in the road moments before, so must have been on the footpath and exited onto the Walsgrave Road,

237 John Boneham was born at Foleshill in 1867, making him thirty-nine years old at the time of the Stoke Park murders. He married Jane Lane in January 1887 and the couple had two children, Harriett and Edith. Boneham died in May 1941.

turning left towards Coventry. The houses between the Old Ball and the footpath entrance had prevented Boneham from noticing the man earlier.

John Boneham had a particular reason for taking in the man's appearance. He had recently had problems with men sleeping rough in his stables, and as a consequence took note of anyone in the vicinity at night or early hours.

The man walking towards him was travelling quickly, bent over, and his hat was pulled down over his face; Boneham later described it as a cap. He was dressed in dark clothing. Boneham noticed the man was carrying something in his right hand under his coat, which was buttoned up. He was twenty-five or twenty-six years old, 5ft 6in or 5ft 7in, and of a slim build. While he was clean shaven, Boneham thought the man looked haggard.

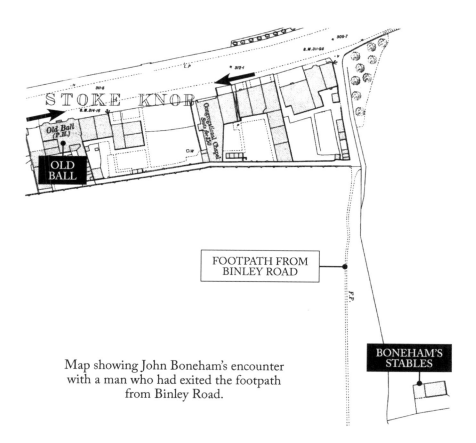

Map showing John Boneham's encounter with a man who had exited the footpath from Binley Road.

John Boneham's view along Stoke Knob; the white arrow indicates his route past the Old Ball on the right.

As the two men were about to pass Boneham said, "Good morning," receiving a brusque "Good morning" in return.

They went their separate ways, with the mysterious man walking briskly toward Coventry, and Boneham down the footpath towards his stables. On arrival he discovered that his fears were unfounded, and nobody had been in his barn. He hitched up his horse and set off for Kenilworth Station, where he had arranged to collect some stones. He thought no more about it until reading reports of the Stoke Park murders the following day.[238]

Was the surly young man seen by John Boneham the same as the

---

238 Deposition of John Boneham in 'Criminal depositions and case papers: MURDER: Taylor' (The National Archives ASSI 13/36).

one who Benjamin Taylor had watched running up the footpath near Stoke Park minutes earlier?

Confirmation seemed to come on 17 January, the day of Mary and Richard's funeral. Benjamin Taylor was in attendance, and while in the church for the service spotted the man he was certain had run up the footpath alongside Stoke Park in the early hours of 11 January. Shortly afterwards, Benjamin thought he recognised the elder man he'd also seen that fateful night.

It was Robert Taylor – Mary Phillips's cousin – and his son Ernest. They were at the funeral not only to pay their respects, but in their roles as undertakers.

Although he didn't know the two men, Benjamin Taylor was certain they were the pair he had seen escaping into the early morning. Later that day he went again to the Police, and told them of his suspicions.[239]

*

Inspector Imber and his team of detectives had also been busy. Aside from the burglary at Spencer Street, they now had reason to suspect that Ernest Taylor was involved with the theft of a bicycle and the subsequent disposing of its various parts.

According to his father, Ernest had since a young boy dealt in bicycle parts, thereby supplementing his income.[240]

And when in February 1906 PC Henry Cox of Coventry City Police followed up information received regarding a bicycle theft in September 1905 and visited cycle repairer Harry Lester at his premises of 91 Spon End, the extent of Ernest Taylor's involvement became apparent.

Lester told the constable that he had been in the Alma Inn on Stoney Stanton Road at the beginning of November the previous year when a man named Walter Eales came in. During the course of conversation Eales asked Mr Lester if he'd be interested in buying

239 Deposition of Benjamin Taylor in 'Criminal depositions and case papers: MURDER: Taylor' (The National Archives ASSI 13/36).
240 Inquest testimony of Robert Taylor in 'Criminal depositions and case papers: MURDER: Taylor' (The National Archives ASSI 13/36).

a bicycle frame, which was at his premises in nearby Jenner Street.

The two men went and took a look, and a price was agreed. They went back to the Alma, and found Eales' brother Tom there drinking with Ernest Taylor.[241] The newcomers asked Mr Lester to look at a pair of wheels belonging to Taylor which might suit the frame; once again they left the pub, and soon a deal was struck for the wheels, including their tyres, and these were taken to Tom Eales' workshop on Stoney Stanton Road, from where Harry Lester took his new purchases and constructed a second-hand bicycle which he intended to sell. Before he could do so PC Cox arrived and took the machine away,[242] heading to the Vernon Cycle Co. on Earl Street, where proprietor Frank Johnstone identified the frame, front forks and tyres as being from a new bicycle he'd sold to a young man named John Lamont back in 1903.

PC Cox telegraphed Mr Lamont, who was now living at Harbury, and the following day he too identified the same parts of the machine which had belonged to him until it was stolen on 16 September 1905.[243]

241 Thomas Eales (1867-1939) was an engineer; his brother Walter (1876-1944), was, like Ernest Taylor, heavily involved in the dealing of bicycle parts around the Stoney Stanton Road, Jenner Street and Queen Street area.

242 Deposition of Harry Lester in 'Criminal depositions and case papers: MURDER: Taylor' (The National Archives ASSI 13/36). Harry Lester, born in 1853, was fifty-two at the time of the bicycle theft. He was married to Ann, the couple having one child, Harry Jr. In 1880 Harry Lester was acquitted of the rape of a young woman named Annie Cooke, who had gone to his warehouse seeking work. Sending an elderly woman on the premises at the time out to locate some silk, Lester locked the door. After telling her mother what had taken place, the Police were called. While Dr Wimberley confirmed after examining Miss Cooke that intercourse had indeed taken place, he found no bruising or marks of any kind which indicated a struggle. The jury returned a verdict that sexual relations had been consensual, the foreman commenting: "I do not think he is a man sufficient to take liberties with her if she resisted him. I think she is as good a man as him." [*Coventry Herald*, 20 February 1880.]

243 Deposition of PC Henry Cox in 'Criminal depositions and case papers: MURDER: Taylor' (The National Archives ASSI 13/36). Henry Cox, born in 1870, was married to Florence, the couple having five children. He was a detective sergeant by the time of the 1911 Census. He died in 1951 aged eighty-one.

In early 1903 James Lamont had bought the bicycle from Frank Johnstone[244] for his brother, John. The family were at that time living at Walsgrave on Sowe. Having paid £6 5s for the machine, Mr Johnstone threw in a cycle lamp as a gift. Inspecting the unexpected addition, John Lamont saw that it had the nameplate 'Vesta' affixed.

During the winter of 1904/05 Lamont was cycling on his way to school when the front wheel stuck in a rut in the hard ground; in addition to a couple of dents to the bicycle as it crashed to the floor, the lamp came detached and fell to the roadside, unseen by its owner. It was only when he arrived at school that Lamont noticed the lamp was missing; too dark to locate it that evening on his way home, the following morning he was more successful and found the missing lamp, with the oil containing part a couple of yards from the top, which was now sporting a few scrapes and dents.

John Lamont continued to use the bicycle and lamp regularly, but in September 1905 left it in the Star Yard in Earl Street, by permission of Frank Johnstone, for fifteen minutes. When he returned, the bicycle was gone.

Having reported the theft at the Police station, Lamont probably didn't expect to see the machine again. It would have been a surprise when he received a telegram from PC Cox on 22 February 1906 asking him to attend the station. When he did, he readily identified most of the cycle sold to Harry Lester by Walter Eales and Ernest Taylor.

And, damningly, he recognised the Stoke Lamp when it was shown to him by Police - despite the black paint and brown paper inserts, the dents were all in the correct place, and the winder which controlled the wick was also bent the same angle as when he had tumbled from the bike.[245]

---

244 Frank Johnstone was just twenty-four years old when he sold the bicycle to James Lamont. He married Beatrice Eaves in 1908.

245 Deposition of John Lamont in 'Criminal depositions and case papers: MURDER: Taylor' (The National Archives ASSI 13/36). John Lamont was born in East Preston, Scotland, in 1888. He was fifteen years old when his elder brother James (twenty-four) bought him a bicycle from Frank Johnstone. John married Mary in 1909, the couple having two children. By 1911 he was running the family farm at Harbury, Droitwich, in place of his infirm father.

Detectives Imber and Bassett had heard enough; they went to Ernest Taylor's workshop in Jenner Street and examined the premises, walking away with another bicycle – later identified as another sold by Frank Johnstone, this time to Mr Langley for use by his salesmen for the firm, Langley, Hickman & Co., a wine merchants of Earl Street.

On 13 November 1905 it was being used by William Green, an agent for the company. He rode it into Castle Street, where he was due to call at the Hare and Hounds. Leaving the bicycle outside under the protection of a small boy and girl - and paying them a penny each for their trouble - Mr Green went inside to conduct his business.[246]

When he returned, both the bicycle and the young children had vanished.

On receiving a request to attend the Police station on 2 February, Mr Green examined the cycle found by Detectives Imber and Cox and, although it was now roughly painted black with Japanning paint, could recognise it as that stolen from his possession three months earlier.[247]

Tom Eales, earning a solid living as an engineer in contrast to his brother's dealing in bicycle parts, told Inspector Imber that he had known Ernest Taylor for several years. He had carried out a number of odd jobs for him from time to time.

In the September of 1905 Taylor had ordered two tools from the engineer, which he called 'scrapers', supposedly for his carpentry work. They were to be eighteen inches long, of chiselled steel, and turned up slightly at each end.

Around a week before Christmas Taylor returned one to Tom Eales, asking him to convert it into an ordinary cold chisel, which meant removing the curved ends. The work was carried out as requested, and Taylor collected. But Mr Eales had kept the curved ends he'd removed, and on Inspector Imber paying a visit handed

---

246 *Birmingham Daily Mail*, 1 March 1906.
247 Deposition of William Green in 'Criminal depositions and case papers: MURDER: Taylor' (The National Archives ASSI 13/36).

them to the officer.

Eales further told the detective that on the afternoon of 10 January Ernest Taylor had been at his workshop and seemed to have had a drink. Suddenly there was a loud gunshot – Taylor had discharged his revolver 'for fun'. They went to the Alma for a drink, Tom returning to his work. A little later Ernest returned to the workshop, and told him landlord Amos Statham had taken the revolver from him.[248]

When Inspector Imber visited the mortuary to inspect the wounds inflicted on Mary and Richard the trimmed metal ends, with a slight curve, were in his pocket. To his eye, they appeared to match perfectly.

*

On 27 January Ernest Taylor was charged with the Spencer Street burglary and the same day transferred to Warwick Gaol to await his trial. As he arrived at Coventry Railway Station with his Police escort, Constable Arthur Daniel, the prisoner was in a jovial mood, and made a startling statement:

> Chief Inspector Imber asked me a question but I refused to answer him. I'm not going to give anyone away, as I am single – the other is a married man with five children. If I suffer for it he will thank me for it some day.

Who was Taylor referring to? Why would he protect someone, when his own life was very much at risk?

The visit to Warwick was a short one; a remand was sought by the Police to enable them an opportunity to speak with Taylor's defence counsel, Sylvester Masser, to warn him that an attempt was being made to link his client with the murders of Richard and Mary Phillips. As a result, the hearing was postponed.

On the return journey Taylor confided in PC Daniel:

> I felt downhearted one day last week, I had a good mind to come it. If I had had any money I should have tossed up to see if I

248 Deposition of Tom Eales in 'Criminal depositions and case papers: MURDER: Taylor' (The National Archives ASSI 13/36).

should do so. Remanded a week, eh! A lot can turn up in a week, can't it.[249]

As it turned out, much information did turn up.

That same day, they sent for Benjamin Taylor and John Boneham to separately attend the Police station to ascertain whether they could identify Ernest Taylor as the young man they had seen in the minutes shortly after the time the murders were probably committed.

Benjamin Taylor was taken into a room, where eight or nine men dressed in dark clothes were waiting in a line. Among them was Ernest Taylor; he was unhesitatingly picked out by the witness.[250]

John Boneham also went to the Police office, and identified Ernest Taylor as the man he had seen walking towards him by the Old Ball inn, having apparently emerged seconds earlier from the footpath leading to the Binley Road.[251]

Inspector Imber and Sergeant Bassett had all the evidence they needed. They told Taylor that the bicycle found in his workshop had been identified as that stolen from William Green in Castle Street in September 1905. Imber then dropped the bombshell, telling the prisoner that the bicycle lamp shown to him a week after the murders was the one left behind in the Phillipses' kitchen by the murderer, warning him:

> You clearly understand me: the lamp I showed you on the 20th January is the one left behind by the murderer at Hawthorn Cottage, and was stolen with this bicycle on the 16th September 1905, and identified?

Taylor coolly replied that while the bicycle and lamp had perhaps been stolen, he wasn't aware of that fact as he had sold them on to a man at Foleshill, who he refused to name.

249 Deposition of PC Arthur Daniel in 'Criminal depositions and case papers: MURDER: Taylor' (The National Archives ASSI 13/36).

250 Deposition of Benjamin Taylor in 'Criminal depositions and case papers: MURDER: Taylor' (The National Archives ASSI 13/36).

251 Deposition of John Boneham in 'Criminal depositions and case papers: MURDER: Taylor' (The National Archives ASSI 13/36).

Inspector Imber then went straight for the kill:

> I told prisoner that two witnesses had identified him as being in the neighbourhood of Stoke Park a little after four o'clock in the morning of the 11th January. Prisoner replied, "Oh yes, will that job come off next March Assizes?"
>
> I then said to prisoner, "You have referred to another man. Consider your position, which is a serious one. You are going to Warwick; tell me the name of the man you refer to, so that I can follow the matter up and clear you if possible."
>
> Prisoner said, "Leave me for a quarter of an hour and come to me again." I returned in half an hour; prisoner said, "I have nothing more to tell you."

The detective's investigation continued. Finally, on Saturday, 10 March, he was ready to formally charge Taylor with the brutal slayings at Stoke Park. In the presence of Chief Constable Charsley, the prisoner was told that he was to be put before the magistrates for the murders of Richard and Mary Phillips.

His response was a derisory "That's a good 'un."[252]

*

While he had been awaiting a turn before the magistrates for burglary, Ernest Taylor now found himself charged with murder, and would appear that same day at Coventry's County Hall.

Since he had been in Police custody, his string of advertisements in the *Coventry Evening Telegraph* had ended. The last in the run came on Thursday 18 January 1906, when a notice appeared offering building, shopfitting and undertaking services. As he had been in custody since 19 January, no renewal had been forthcoming.

Meanwhile, at Stoke Park efforts to wipe away all memory of the murders gathered pace. Five days after Ernest Taylor was charged with the killings, the *Coventry Evening Telegraph* reported:

> The name of Hawthorn Cottage, the scene of the tragedy, has been altered to Beulah House. The house has been renovated, and is at

252 Deposition of Inspector William Imber in 'Criminal depositions and case papers: MURDER: Taylor' (The National Archives ASSI 13/36).

present undergoing structural alteration, the greenhouse, which occupied the entire length of the rear of the dwelling, being removed to make room for more bedroom accommodation.[253]

Hawthorn Cottage had been bequeathed by Mary to Percy Eld, her friend of sixteen years, regular gardener and occasional house-sitter.[254] He had not waited long to remodel the house to his own specifications.

253 *Coventry Evening Telegraph*, 15 March 1906.
254 Deposition of Percy William Eld in 'Criminal depositions and case papers: MURDER: Taylor' (The National Archives ASSI 13/36).

6.

MR MASSER
ADDRESSES THE JURY

As would be expected, a large crowd gathered by the courthouse to catch a glimpse of the prisoner as he was brought before the magistrates from Warwick Gaol. Guarded by Police officers, Taylor spoke to people he recognised on the way to the cells, and on being placed in the dock turned his back on the magistrates to survey the spectators, smiling at those he knew. He caught sight of his father, Robert Taylor, and gave him a nod.[255]

One newspaper, commenting that his was a familiar face in the court given his earlier appearances there in relation to the housebreaking and bicycle stealing cases, described the prisoner as wearing a dark coat with velvet collar, and a stand-up collar. He appeared older than his tender years, and bore the appearance of "a male indoor servant, or gentleman's gardener."[256]

Proceedings during his first appearance in the dock were brief:

POLICE COURT PROCEEDINGS

At Coventry Police Court this morning a further stage was reached in the development of the Stoke Park tragedy, when Charles Ernest Robert Taylor, carpenter, of 16, Spencer Street, the young man who already stood committed for trial on separate charges of burglary and larceny, was brought up in custody and charged with the wilful murder of Mr and Mrs Richard Phillips.

Two separate charges were preferred against the accused. The

255 *Daily News*, 19 March 1906.
256 *Daily News*, 12 March 1906.

An enhanced photograph of Charles Ernest Robert Taylor
from the Midland Daily Telegraph, 10 March 1906

first set forth that he "did on the night of the 10th or morning of the 11th of January last, at Hawthorn Cottage, Stoke Park, feloniously, wilfully and of his malice aforethought, kill and murder one Richard Phillips." The second was that he "also at the same time and place did kill and murder one Mary Phillips."

The police court was fully crowded, and the gangways were thronged by the usual curious spectators before the commencement of the business this morning. The magistrates present were Ald. Marriott (chairman), Dr Lynes, Messrs Rowland Hill, Edgar Turrall, and W. Pridmore. The prisoner Taylor had been brought over from Warwick Prison by train that morning, and driven up to the police station in an omnibus in the usual way.

On his name being called he stepped up into the dock accompanied by a prison warder. Taylor wore a dark overcoat, buttoned tightly across the chest, and stood with his feet wide apart and his hands behind his back. The accompanying illustration gives a good portrait of his strongly marked features, except that since his detention in custody he had grown a short beard, contrasting with his dark hair, and just long enough to obscure the lines of the jaw, without obscuring the mouth.[257]

There was little evidence given on the first day. Thomas Tickner, the husband of Rose Tickner who had looked into the lit windows of Hawthorn Cottage as the couple made their way to their home on Stoke Green late on the evening of 10 January, was a surveyor and architect, and it was he who had been called to produce various plans for the magistrates' hearing, and gave evidence as to the layout and measurements of Hawthorn Cottage.[258]

A list of exhibits to be shown at the trial was prepared, with certain items now acquiring an identifying name, and proved extensive:

1. Stoke Lamp
2. Lamont's bicycle (No. 2 Lamont)
3. Cycle lamp and vessel found in prisoner's workshop
4. Green's bicycle (No. 1 Langley)
5. Lamp wicks
6. 3 silver watches & gold chain found in bedroom at Hawthorn Cottage
7. Box containing jewellery (ditto)
8. Human tooth and nail (do)
9. Purse containing 4/3 ½ (do)
10. Bedclothes (do)
11. Pair female drawers (do)
12. Cash box (do)
12a. Pocket knife (do)
13. Cloth covered with human excrement found in fire grate in sitting room (Stoke)
14. Bottle containing home made wine
15. Two copies of 'B'ham Daily Mail' Jan 11 and 12 found on floor put through letter slot
15a. Calendar
16. Bottle containing brandy found in kitchen (Hawthorn Cottage)
17. Pantry window and catch
18. Two glue brushes & two Japan brushes found in prisoner's workshop

257 *Midland Daily Telegraph*, 10 March 1906.
258 Deposition of Thomas Tickner in 'Criminal depositions and case papers: MURDER: Taylor' (The National Archives ASSI 13/36).

19. Samples of paper (ditto)
20. Two Japan bottles (do)
21. Tin containing black paint (do)
22. Six steel chisels (do)
23. Bottle containing turpentine (do)
24. Bottle containing Coleshill cycle lamp oil (do)
25. Mirror (do)
26. Two cycle lamps (Quail)
27. Two jemmy ends (Eales)
28. Jemmy (produced for Dr Loudon to compare with wounds)
29. Revolver and cartridges
30. Bottle of paraffin from workshop
31. Clothing taken from bodies of Mr & Mrs Phillips
32. Prisoner's clothing
33. County Court summons
34. Two drawers from looking glass
35. No. 3 Elton bicycle
36. Memo tablet
37. Book *James Cycles 1906*[259]

With just a little further evidence being heard, the hearing was then adjourned. Taylor turned and liaised with his counsel:

Prisoner listened to the brief and formal proceedings with an air of imperturbability, exchanged a few words with his legal representative, Mr G. Davies of Messrs Hughes and Masser, and when informed by Ald. Marriott that he would be reprimanded spoke up sharply and said, "Well, I wish to say, gentlemen, I had nothing to do with it." He apparently would have added more, but was silenced with a gesture from Mr Davies, and, colouring up slightly, as though with momentary annoyance, was tapped on the shoulder by the dock officers and stepped downstairs quietly.[260]

The magistrates' hearing would be resumed, adjourned and resumed again over the coming weeks, with a myriad of witnesses taking the stand to give their evidence. But it was the testimony of

259 Criminal depositions and case papers: MURDER: Taylor (The National Archives ASSI 13/36).
260 *Midland Daily Telegraph*, 10 March 1906.

Dr John Loudon as to the nature of the injuries inflicted on Richard and Mary Phillips which sent a chill through those present:

First of all I found the woman's linen garment encircling her neck, chin and mouth, having been twice round and the first round having been knotted. On removing it I found that it had exercised such compression as to flatten and turn downwards and outwards the lower lip. The use of the garment would tend to prevent the woman making any noise, and it might interfere with her breathing.

The wounds on the woman consisted of four principal ones. There was a wound No. 1 on the right-hand side of the forehead. It was running almost vertically, was two inches long and gaping, and right through to the skull. The second wound was in a similar position on the other side of the forehead. It was two inches long, gaping and to the bone throughout it, whole length. The 3rd wound commenced at the inner angle of the right eye, ran upwards and to the left, terminating about an inch above the middle of the left eyebrow. This wound was 2¼ inches long, and was gaping and to the bone throughout its whole length. The fourth wound was on the top of the head. It almost completely detached a circular piece of scalp, having a diameter of three inches. The skull immediately underneath was fractured and depressed.

All the wounds must have been occasioned by considerable force and a heavy weapon. Either the first or fourth described wound could have been mortal.

The shape of the first three wounds was curved. The jemmy produced to me now was shown to me by Chief Insp. Imber. It did not well fit the wounds, its curve being too acute. Apart from the acuteness of the curve of the jemmy supplied to me by Chief Insp. Imber, the first three wounds are such as might have been caused by the curved end of a jemmy. In my opinion the fourth wounds could have been used by a similar instrument used horizontally.

These four wounds were all the wounds on the woman. There were no other marks of violence on the body.

With regard to the dead man, I found sixteen wounds. Beginning with the face, the first wound was on the left side of the chin, a flesh wound 2½ inches long fracturing the lower jaw. The wound No. 2 was immediately below No. 1, two thirds of an inch long. No. 3 ran from the right side of the nose downwards and outwards across the cheek, was three inches long and to the bone, where there was bone. No. 4 was a wound above the right eye, on the forehead, was three inches long running vertically and to the bone throughout its extend. This wound was bifurcated below, and appeared to have been produced by two blows almost in the same spot. The fifth wound was almost on the same level as the fourth, but to the right. It was 2¼ inches long, and to the bone throughout its extent and gaping, as indeed was No. 4. No. 6 was on the same level and similar in direction to No. 5, was one inch long – to the bone and gaping. No. 7 was behind the hinder ends of Nos. 4 and 5, running almost transversely for 2½ inches to the bone – gaping. No. 8 was a little behind and to the right of No. 7, was two inches long, to the bone and gaping. No. 9 commenced near the minor end of No. 8, and ran backwards 3¼ inches to the bone throughout its extent, and gaping. No. 10 began close to the hinder end of No. 9, ran outwards, slightly forwards for two inches, was to the bone throughout its extent and gaping. No. 11 was a wound between Nos. 8 and 10, was one and a half inches long, to the bone and gaping. No. 12 was behind all the wounds previously described, and slightly nearer the middle of the head, was one inch long, to the bone and gaping. No. 13 was slightly forward of No. 12, on the left side of the head, one inch long, to the bone and gaping. No. 14 was a wound above the left eyebrow and parallel with it – 2¼ inches long, to the bone and gaping. No. 15 was a wound between Nos. 13 and 14, slightly more to the right, was 3½ inches long, dipping at the scalp. No. 16 was a wound similarly situated below the left eye, 1½ inches long and underneath it was a fracture for the cheekbone.

At the back of the right arm was a wound an inch long, a slight wound on the right elbow and a slight wound in the back of the right hand. There was some bruising at the back of the left hand, and the left little fingernail was off.

Some of the wounds were probably inflicted when the man was standing up; others I think must have been delivered after he was down. It was quite impossible for him to received all these blows and remain standing. Death would have ensured in a very short time, either a few seconds or one minute or two.

The deaths might have happened two-three or four days before I made my examination. The post mortem rigidity was fully established, and had not begun to decline and decomposition hand commenced.

Ernest Taylor at the magistrates' hearing.
from Lloyds' Weekly Newspaper, 1 April 1906.

The wounds on the man and woman might have been produced by one or more instruments, but could have been produced by one instrument.

Cross examined, Dr Loudon added his thoughts on how the attacks had been inflicted:

With regard to the wounds on the woman, wounds Nos. 1 and 2 were vertical and I should think were inflicted whilst she was in an upright position by a person standing in front of her and striking downwards. The third wound would appear to have been inflicted while the head at least was upright, and the fourth wound might have been inflicted whilst she was falling.

From the blood on the wall I think a small artery had spurted. There was some squirting from a small vessel on to the wall facing the end of the bed, close to where the woman's body was found.

The wounds of a curved shape were mainly on the forehead. They were fairly clean cut wounds. After she fell there was evidently considerable dripping of blood from the wounds.

Referring to the man, there were five or six wounds on the scalp in a vertical or back-to-front direction. The five wounds I refer to might have been caused by a man standing in front him or by a man standing behind him. I could not in the case of the man credit any one blow with being the fatal one. The other eleven blows were more horizontal, or less vertical.

Practically all the wounds have an indication of curving. In the case of the man the majority of the wounds were clean cut, to the bone. The wounds on the man were, generally speaking, of quite such a severe character as those on the woman.

The body of the man had been moved, and the head and left shoulder pushed under the bed. When the man had fallen there would be oozing of blood from all the wounds. On the walls near the body of the man there were spots of blood. From the position, character and number of the wounds of the man, there would be a considerable spotting of blood.

There were a few ounces of blood near the body of the woman, and there were evidences that prior to the removal of the body [to the mortuary] there had been blood under the body of the man. I should think the man had put his arm up, and received a little damage.

I should think under the conditions that rigor mortis might have set in at the end of about twelve hours, and might possibly last three, four or five days.[261]

Detective Inspector William Imber told the court how he thought the attack had unfolded:

My opinion is that the woman was struck about three blows in quick succession; that she fell and was caught on the bedpost by her nightdress, a fourth downwards blow was struck when she was in the position in which she was found. From the fourth blow she would bleed freely.

With regards to the wounds on the husband, I should think from my observations that some may have been inflicted whilst he was in bed, some whilst he was out of bed and some after he was dead.

261 Deposition of Dr John Loudon in 'Criminal depositions and case papers: MURDER: Taylor' (The National Archives ASSI 13/36).

From the fact that the fingernail was missing, it looks as if he put one arm up to protect himself. I think Mr Phillips fell by the night commode, [and] received numerous blows afterwards and there was splashing of blood on the night commode and curtains near it.

I should think the body of the man had been rolled over and the legs extended towards the window after he was dead. There would naturally be a considerable amount of bleeding, and I think the moving of the body would possibly bring blood on the hands.

From the nature of the blows I should not expect to find much blood on the murderer's clothing – there might be some. There was no blood on the chest of drawers or cash box. I think from this the cash box had been opened before the murder was committed.

In my opinion the greenhouse door was not opened by the murderer. The £16 10s was secreted under some old pots in the portion of the greenhouse behind the unoccupied bedroom.[262]

Other witnesses gave interesting testimony.

The young men involved in the saga of the stolen bicycles told of their part in the story.

Frederick Green, an employee of Goodwin & Co. Export Merchants of Birmingham, testified how the company had supplied cycle lamps to the Vernon Cycle Company during 1902/03, and that the so-called 'Stoke Lamp' was indeed one of theirs – albeit with the 'Vesta' nameplate removed, and the plated finished now roughly painted black.[263]

Ellen Taylor, Ernest's mother, said that her son had not been to Hawthorn Cottage since he was two years old, and hadn't seen Mrs Phillips – his second cousin – at all since he was six.

Her apparent fearful reaction to being shown the Stoke Lamp was due to her being ill, not due to any guilty knowledge, she claimed.[264]

The renowned forensic chemist Dr Alfred Bostock Hill, at that

262 Deposition of Inspector William Imber in 'Criminal depositions and case papers: MURDER: Taylor' (The National Archives ASSI 13/36).

263 Deposition of Frederick Green in 'Criminal depositions and case papers: MURDER: Taylor' (The National Archives ASSI 13/36).

264 Deposition of Ellen Taylor in 'Criminal depositions and case papers: MURDER: Taylor' (The National Archives ASSI 13/36).

time Professor of Hygiene and Public Health at Birmingham University but formerly its Professor of Chemistry, appeared and told the court of his exmaination of a number of items related to the case, including the Stoke Lamp and wick, paper and glue, and a tin of black paint found in Ernest's Taylor Jenner Street workshop.

The forensic expert looked at the petroleum wick in the Stoke Lamp, and found it was identical to three similar wicks found at Jenner Street. Similarly, samples of brown paper in Taylor's possession were matches to the paper glued into the insides of the lamp to block its side-lights; microscopically and chemically they were identical. Oil contained in a bottle labelled Coleshill Cycle Lamp Oil was exactly the same as that used in the Stoke Lamp.[265]

The magistrates were impressed, but nevertheless retired for half an hour to debate the evidence before committing Ernest Taylor to trial for murder.

On being told he was being sent to Warwick to appear at the forthcoming Assizes, Taylor replied "Very well," and was made to remain the dock for a considerable time while the depositions of some forty-one witnesses were read over to him.[266]

The inquest into the deaths, held at the Union Workhouse before Charles Webb Iliffe, was also not without incident.

James Harsent, a warder at Warwick Gaol, appeared to testify that Ernest Taylor had gained 23lbs in weight since being taken into custody – almost one-and-a-half stones.[267] Prison food evidently agreed with the prisoner.

265 Deposition of Dr Alfred Bostock Hill in 'Criminal depositions and case papers: MURDER: Taylor' (The National Archives ASSI 13/36). Bostock Hill (1854-1932) was the son of Dr Alfred Hill, Medical Officer for Health for Birmingham, and was educated at the city's King Edward School, New Street and then Queen's College. At the age of twenty-two he was appointed public analyst for Warwickshire. He became Professor of Chemistry at Queen's in 1879, and later Professor of Hygiene and Public Health at Birmingham. He married Elizabeth Barber in 1883, the couple having two children.

266 *Birmingham Daily Gazette*, 10 May 1906.

267 Inquest testimony of James Harsent in 'Criminal depositions and case papers: MURDER: Taylor' (The National Archives ASSI 13/36). Job title from trade directories and 1901 Census.

More seriously, the coroner's court was in uproar when witness Benjamin Taylor gave evidence as to the two men he saw on the Binley Road in the very early hours of 11 January.

He had identified the younger man at Coventry Police Station, and now said that the elder man was in court that day.

Ernest's solicitor Mr Masser asked Robert Taylor, until then sitting comfortably at the back of the room, to stand up.

The witness excitedly said he did not identify him as the man; that was a job for the Police. Nevertheless, he addressed Robert Taylor and said that he had every resemblance to the man he had seen on the Binley Road.

The response was a withering "If you say I am the man you are a liar."

Benjamin Taylor complained that he was only there to serve justice; he was as sure that Robert Taylor was the elder man he had seen as he was that Ernest was the younger.[268]

Despite this angry exchange of views as to the identity of the second man, the coroner's jury were as to no doubt as to Ernest Taylor's involvement. After a scant few minutes' deliberation they declared that they were

> unanimous in their opinion that the prisoner Charles Ernest Robert Taylor did with aforethought kill and slay Richard Phillips and Mary Phillips during the night of the 10th day of January, 1906, at Hawthorn Cottage, Stoke Park, in the city of Coventry.

With typical cynicism, the prisoner muttered, "They must be a set of fools then."[269] He was removed from the dock and returned to Warwick.

*

For now, Inspector Imber and Police Surgeon John Loudon returned to their duties.

---

268 *Lancashire Daily Post*, 11 May 1906.
269 *Leamington Spa Courier*, 18 May 1906.

On 16 July Imber appeared before the magistrates to testify in the case of Winifred Cronin, a young woman who had been drunk and disorderly in Gosford Street. The detective testified that it was her first offence, and as such she was asked to sign the pledge. She declined, saying, "I certainly will not sign the pledge until I feel so inclined."[270]

At the same hearing Imber gave evidence in the case against Charles Williams, a machinist of Sherbourne Street, who had not only stolen a bicycle but had assaulted PC Nicholls when questioned about it, cutting the constable's eye after punching him in the face. It transpired that Williams had twice been thrown out of a public house that day due to his inebriation. In court he expressed remorse, saying he had been drinking heavily recently – in fact, he hadn't been sober for three weeks.[271]

There must have been something in the air that summer. In August Imber appeared at the Police Court as magistrates heard the case against Joseph Jacox, a bricklayer of no fixed abode, who had been found by PC Chaffer lying drunk on the pavement in Spon Street. The officer lifted him to his feet, whereupon Jacox attempted to run off only to fall flat on his face. Imber told the court this was his forty-sixth appearance for similar offences, and although he had not before the court since May 1905 it was probably because he was out of town. Jacox was fined 10s with costs.[272]

That same month Dr John Loudon was called to examine the body of a man who been discovered dead on the floor of his home on Leicester Street. William Chetwyn had seen his neighbour, Samuel Arnold, on the morning of 18 August and he appeared well. That afternoon one of Chetwyn's children went to see whether Arnold

270 *Coventry Evening Telegraph*, 16 July 1906. Winifred Cronin was thirty-five at the time of her arrest. She married John Payne in 1910 and had no further brushes with the law, passing away in 1915.

271 *Coventry Herald*, 21 July 1906.

272 *Coventry Evening Telegraph*, 22 August 1906. Joseph Jacox was born in 1855. Magistrates heard at an earlier case – in August 1893 – how he was "alright so long as he kept from the drink", but when drunk continually assaulted his wife, Lucy. [*Coventry Herald*, 18 August 1893.] She died at Hatton Lunatic Asylum in 1903, no doubt worn out by the constant abuse.

needed any errands doing, and found him collapsed on the floor. The child ran to fetch a neighbour, Joseph Denny, who in turn went and found nearby PC Silcocks in the Burges around four o'clock.[273]

Samuel Arnold was well known to the Police – not least for his infamous bare-knuckle bout on Hearsall Common in 1881 which resulted in the death of his opponent.[274] Dr Loudon was sent for, and after an examination of the body concluded death was probably from syncope.[275]

At the inquest the following week Samuel Arnold's daughter Alice – who would go on to become Coventry's first female mayor – told Coroner Iliffe that her father was heavily addicted to drink; he had complained of heart trouble and dropsy, and two weeks before his death he had fallen down the stairs. This resulted in a visit to the hospital, where he was treated for bruised ribs. Since that day he had been unable to work, instead lying propped up in bed. Loudon told the coroner that he suspect syncope following latent heart disease, and a verdict was returned to that effect.[276]

Dr John Loudon continued his duties as Police Surgeon for many years to come. He retired as medical attendant to the Coventry Provident Dispensary in 1912,[277] and as Police Surgeon in September 1914.[278] The following year he retired as medical consultant to Coventry Brigade, having served them for seventeen years.[279]

Loudon then fully retired from practice and left Coventry for good, settling in North Wales at Bettws-y-Coed. He died there in May 1917.[280]

273 *Kenilworth Advertiser*, 25 August 1906.
274 See *The Watchmaker's Revenge* by Adam Wood (2021).
275 *Coventry Evening Telegraph*, 18 August 1906.
276 *Kenilworth Advertiser*, 25 August 1906.
277 *Coventry Evening Telegraph*, 23 May 1912.
278 *Coventry Evening Telegraph*, 25 September 1914.
279 *Coventry Evening Telegraph*, 18 November 1915.
280 *Coventry Evening Telegraph*, 20 May 1917.

7.

A GAP IN THE MESH

The Warwickshire Summer Assizes opened on Friday, 20 July 1906. The calendar was an unusually heavy one, with twenty-two cases to be heard before Hon. Bernard John Seymour, Lord Coleridge.[281]

Sworn in as the Grand Jury were Colonel Rowland Beech as foreman, with Colonel Woollcombe-Adams, Major Gregory, Major Chesshyre Molyneux, Major Gisborne, Major Armstrong accompanied by Messrs Lakin, Lucas, Munts, Chance, Caldecott, Gerard, Cay, Booth, Everett, Thorne, Hatherell, Thursfield, Wood and Flavel. From this group juries of twelve would be selected for each case.

On the first morning the Court heard the cases against Benjamin Allcock, a thirty-two year old groom, who pleaded Guilty to obtaining a cheque valued £1 10s by false pretences. He was sentenced to a month's imprisonment.

It was a gentle start to proceedings.

Next up was thirty year old Rose Chandler, who pleaded Guilty to the concealment of the birth of her child on 4 May that year. The baby had died, but no marks had been found upon its body, nor

---

281 Born in 1851, Bernard John Seymour Coleridge, 2nd Baron Coleridge was educated at Eton and Trinity College, Oxford. He was called to the Bar at Middle Temple in 1877. Coleridge was elected Member of Parliament for Sheffield Attercliffe in the 1885 General Election and held the seat until 1894. He became a QC in 1892 and served as a Judge of the High Court of Justice from 1907 to 1923. Before this, Lord Coleridge served as Commissioner of Assize, and it was in the role that he presided over the trial of Ernest Taylor at Warwick.

Shire Hall, Warwick.

any indication of wrongdoing on the part of Ms Chandler. She was bound over in the sum of £10.

Before lunch the jury heard evidence against four men – Edward Tompkins (thirty years old), Reuben Plummer (thirty-three), James Walker (twenty-three) and George Turner (thirty) – who were charged with breaking into the Coventry home of George Franks and stealing a gold chain and seal, a gold bracelet and around £18 in cash.[282]

Other prisoners awaiting trial included Ellen Hopkins, a servant charged with murdering her baby daughter at Studley the previous month; Thomas Bicknell, a Warwick gardener who had attempted to kill himself; and Emma Jeffcoat, a servant charged with attempted arson at Kenilworth.[283]

The most serious case on the schedule – the Stoke Park murders levelled at Charles Ernest Robert Taylor – was slated to start on the Monday, 23 July.

When the day came the Court was, as anticipated, extremely crowded. One newspaper described how

282 *Leamington Spa Courier*, 20 July 1906.
283 *Leamington Spa Courier*, 27 July 1906.

the quaint little circular court at Warwick accommodated but a small proportion of the large number of people who gathered round the Shire Hall in the hope of being able to gain admission to the hearing.[284]

By the time the jurors had been called into the box, at a quarter to eleven, all available seats had been quickly snapped up, with a number of ladies occupying those in the front rows. There were more reporters from the numerous newspapers than places allocated to them, so some had to encroach on the space reserved for counsel.[285]

Mr Yorke Stanger KC, MP[286] appeared for the prosecution on behalf of the Treasury, assisted by Mr J.J. Parfitt[287] and Mr Henry Maddocks.[288]

Mr S.R. Masser,[289] Coventry solicitor, had instructed Mr H.H.

284 *Coventry Observer*, 27 July 1906.

285 *Midland Daily Telegraph*, 23 July 1906.

286 Henry Yorke Stanger (1849-1929) was called to the Bar in 1874, serving as a Revising Barrister for Warwickshire between 1892 and 1894. He became Queen's Council the following year. Stanger served as Recorder of Nottingham from 1909 to 1911, and as a County Court Judge from 1910.

287 James John Alexander Parfitt was called to the Bar in 1887, becoming QC in 1908, and served as a County Court judge from 1918 until his death eight years later. Before his legal career he had been a keen cricketer, bowling fast-medium in fourteen first-class cricket matches during a career that spanned from 1881 to 1885 for Surrey and Somerset. He later appeared for Warwickshire in a second-class match.

288 Sir Henry Maddocks (1871-1931) qualified as a solicitor in 1893, at the age of twenty-two. He worked as managing clerk at a practice in Birmingham and Coventry, and concurrently served as clerk to the magistrates of Coleshill Petty Sessions. Maddocks became a barrister of the Inner Temple in 1904, and practiced on the Midland judicial circuit.

289 Sylvester Richard Masser (1848-1922) was born at Foleshill and educated at a private school near Windsor. After being admitted a solicitor he initially had offices in Earl Street, and then Little Park Street. Masser was later appointed Deputy Coroner to Charles Webb Iliffe. When he died in 1922, Major Woollcombe-Adams, then Chairman of the County Police Court and who had sat on the jury in the Taylor trial, commented that he was "the doyen of the legal profession who practiced in the Court. He had been connected with it for a long time - nearly half a century - and during that period he had built up a most enviable reputation as a sound lawyer and a Tenacious and fighting advocate." [*Coventry Standard*, 24 November 1922.]

Joy to act as Ernest's defence counsel.[290]

When Taylor appeared in the dock it was seen that he had changed his appearance since his turn in front of the Coventry magistrates; gone was the sandy beard, with a small moustache now adorning his top lip.[291]

One reporter, perhaps mindful of his readers' eagerness for fine detail, described how the prisoner was

> neatly dressed in black with a white bow. He looked the picture of health. His ruddy cheeks looked almost sunburnt. He gazed round the Court and the crowded galleries with the utmost complacency. In answer to the Clerk of the Assizes he replied to the four indictments "Not Guilty" in clear tones.[292]

Mr Stanger, opening the case, reminded the jury that they had to put our of their minds anything they had read or heard in relation to the case before today – surely an impossible task given the immense newspaper coverage since Taylor had been arrested six months earlier.[293]

Over three days the many witnesses appeared and repeated their testimony given at the magistrates' hearing and the inquest. Immediately after Benjamin Taylor said again that he thought the second man he saw

Mr Yorke Stanger

running into Stoke Park was Robert Taylor, prosecution counsel Mr Stanger startled the court by telling Lord Justice Coleridge that "a threat was used towards this witness before going into the

290 Henry Holmes Joy (1875-1939) was the son of a Tamworth doctor, and was educated at Sherborne and Trinity Hall, Cambridge. He was called to the Bar in 1900, serving the Midlands Circuit with distinction before taking silk in 1927.

291 *Leamington Spa Courier*, 27 July 1906.

292 *Birmingham Gazette and Express*, 24 July 1906.

293 *Leamington Spa Courier*, 27 July 1906.

witness box. I don't like to say from whom it proceeds. Shall I ask the witness if such a threat was used?"

Frustratingly for the modern reader, as well as Mr Stanger, Lord Coleridge said it would be better for the matter to be dropped.[294]

Who had made the threat to Benjamin Taylor?

On the third day Ernest Taylor himself was put in the dock by Mr Joy. In the course of a barrage of questioning last three and a half hours, he said that he had never spoken to Mary Phillips. He was taken to Hawthorn Cottage when he was about six years old, and had never been back since. He had never seen or spoken to Richard Phillips, but had once asked his mother "who that man was who had married Mrs Waterfall?"

He told the Court that on the night of the murders he had arrived home at Spencer Street before midnight, and saw that his parents had gone to bed. As he had no key, and not wishing to awaken his father, he went to the outside closet and fell asleep there. After an hour or so he woke very cold, so got up and went to the Jenner Street workshop, where he lay on the bench to sleep. He noticed it was two o'clock in the morning. He woke again at six, and on going home he saw the back door was open, his father washing at the kitchen sink.

He claimed the first he heard of the murders was on the evening of the discovery. The following day his father asked if he would help with the funeral, to which he agreed.

Taylor admitted that he suspected the bicycles he handled had been stolen, but he knew no details. He had sold the parts before the end of 1905, including the lamp, but couldn't say who had bought them.

Mr Stanger rose to cross examine, and a frisson of excitement ran through the court. The prosecutor highlighted the fact that Ernest had claimed to arrive home at 11.35pm, and his father had told the inquest that he had arrived at 11.33 – a coincidence, replied the prisoner, not a matter of collusion.

It was time for the closing speeches.

294 *Birmingham Gazette and Express*, 24 July 1906.

Mr Stanger spoke for over an hour, and reminded the jury that the prosecution did not suggest that the murderer – whoever he was – went to Hawthorn Cottage with the intention of killing the old couple. Rather, the motive was robbery, and it was expected to be a comparatively straightforward enterprise. Instead, said Stanger, the burglar had been interrupted in his efforts by Mr and Mrs Phillips waking up, and decided he had to carry out the awful crimes for which the prisoner was now before them.[295]

Taylor in the dock.

Defence counsel Mr Joy rose to deliver a powerful closing speech, drawing attention to the fact that the evidence regarding the lamp and the cycle parts – not to mention the supposed identification of the prisoner by Benjamin Taylor and John Boneham – was inconclusive and uncertain. He

> asked the jury whether the accused, if he was the murderer, was likely to leave in his workshop the oil, the brown paper, the wick, the cycle black, and all the other things that could be collected to trace the cycle lamp to him? It could not be suggested that the accused had concealed any of these things.
>
> Mr Joy submitted that there was some doubt that the murders were committed on the night of the 10th January, and if that date was wrong the whole fabric built up by the prosecution collapsed.
>
> He said there was another question to which he invited the jury's attention. Was it conceivable – was it credible – that the accused,

295 *Leamington Spa Courier*, 27 July 1906.

a mere lad of twenty-one years, if he murdered these poor old people, could have attended their funeral in the capacity of undertaker only a few days after his crime?

Mr H.H. Joy

That little bedroom at Hawthorn Cottage was a shambles, and the doctor called for the prosecution said that whatever length the weapon was, the person who wielded it and smote those awful blows would have received bloodstains on his hands and clothing. That was a matter the prosecution had to smooth away.

It had been stated in evidence that prisoner washed himself before he sat down to breakfast at home. Let a man be as diabolically cunning as was possible, would they find a young lad who the devilish ingenuity – after returning to Jenner Street and scouring himself, as was suggested – to go to his home in Spencer Street and to be so thoughtful as to wash himself again in the presence of his parents before sitting down to breakfast?[296]

At this, the Court adjourned.

Whilst Ernest Taylor had appeared calm throughout, his mother and father were obviously coping with shredded nerves.

At last, it was time for the judge's summing up:

> The silence was almost oppressive when Lord Coleridge turned to the jury and commended his wonderful review and analysis of a most intricate and complex case. In quiet, deliberate tones, he reminded the jurors that they were empanelled to discharged the most solemn duty which any body of men in this world could be called upon to perform.
>
> Complicated and difficult as the case was in many respects, he continued, the peculiarity about it was that the prosecution did not attempt to prove the prisoner to be guilty by the evidence of eye-witnesses, or by any direct confession of the accused. The case, therefore, must rest, and rest entirely, upon what was

296 *Nuneaton Observer*, 27 July 1906.

called circumstantial evidence, given by the witnesses called by the prosecution, and confirmed and strengthened by statements alleged to have been made by the accused.

Circumstantial evidence varied in each case. It might amount to evidence giving rise to nothing more that the barest suspicion. It might, perhaps, be likened to a network which might absolutely prevent all change of escape. But that depended upon there being no gaps in the meshes, and if there were a large gap in the net the whole of the net became valueless for the purpose of preventing escape.

Lord Coleridge went on to give a brief summary of the case for the prosecution and defence.

The theory of the prosecution was that on the night of January 10, or in the early morning of the 11th, the prisoner broke into Hawthorn Cottage for the sake of plunder. It was said that a stolen bicycle and lamp were traced to his possession, and that the lamp attached to the bicycle when it was stolen was left behind after the murder was committed. The accused, so it was said, was seen on the early morning of the 11th coming in the direction of Hawthorn Cottage, and in more or less close proximity to it. The prisoner did not, in fact, sleep at home of the night of the murder.

It was said that he had in his possession, shortly before the murder committed, two instruments of iron and steel of a peculiar character. It was said that the wounds inflicted on the deceased were such as would have been inflicted by one or other of these weapons.

It was also said for the prosecution that the accused made statements to the Police which were inconsistent with his innocence.

For the defence it was said, and rightly said, that they have a number of coincidences, curious and suspicious, but such coincidences might fall far short of absolutely proof, and after all absolute proof was the only proof on which they ought to act.

It was said that the prisoner accounted in a sufficiently satisfactorily manner for his movements during that time, and there was no satisfactory manner for his movements during that time, and there was no satisfactory proof upon which the jury could act that the accused was in the neighbourhood of Stoke Park during the time in question.

It was contended that it was not proved that the parts of the cycle said to be Lamont's with which prisoner was dealing were, in fact, parts of the bicycle which was stolen with the lamp on it. It was also said that there was no evidence that prisoner knew at the time that the cycle parts were stolen.

Further, it was said that with regard to the prisoner's statements, though they might appear at first sight to bear an incriminating aspect, they were accounted for by the fact that the prisoner was at that time defending himself against another charge.

It was said in conclusion that no blood was found on the accused's clothing, and there was no evidence of the destruction or cleansing of any clothes by him.

For two hours the Commissioner had under review the evidence with regard to the Lamont cycle and lamp, and the tools made for the accused by Eales.

Just after noon Lord Coleridge turned his attention to the movements of the prisoner on the night of the murder, and the evidence of Benjamin Taylor and Boneham, who said they saw him near Hawthorn Cottage about four o'clock in the morning.

Dealing with the evidence of Benjamin Taylor, who said he saw two men, the accused and his father, his lordship said it must be stated in fairness to the prisoner's father that no suggestion was made during the case by the prosecution that the prisoner's father was implicated in the case, or that he was near Hawthorn Cottage on the morning of January 11. Yet the witness Taylor said he had a better opportunity of seeing the older man than the younger. He [Lord Coleridge] made no suggestion against the truthfulness and candour of the witness Taylor, but the only question was whether it was more than an ordinary suspicion that the younger man he had a momentary glimpse of was the accused.

John Boneham said that a few minutes later he saw the caused going along a footpath towards the Walsgrave Road. Boneham said he had reason to carefully observe the man, because a man had been sleeping in his stables. Was he the younger man, who, according to the witness Taylor, ran away when met on the Binley Road?

Benjamin Taylor said the young man was wearing a 'Trilby' hat, but Boneham said he was wearing a cap. He (the Commissioner) had asked the witnesses about the time between the two meetings, thinking that perhaps accused had time to change his

Lord Justice Coleridge.

hat for a cap worn by the other man, but the witness said the elder man was wearing a bowler hat.

That was the evidence, and his lordship remarked that he could not alter it or assist the jury in considering it.

Lord Coleridge went on to the point out what he termed the difficulties of the prosecution. One of their greatest difficulties was that there was not a speck of blood found upon any of the clothes of the accused. If the prisoner struck the blows that killed the old people, the inference was irresistible that some portion of his clothing must have borne stains of blood. It was hinted that prisoner might have destroyed his clothes when his returned to his workshop, but there was no evidence of destruction.

The prosecution had suggested that there was an accomplice in the crime. If the accomplice struck the blows, the prosecution must, in order to convict the prisoner, prove that he was a consenting party to the murder. The fact that two men were engaged in an unlawful enterprise, say burglary, the fact that one was aiding and abetting the other in that purpose did not make that man a murderer if the other man, in a sudden fit of passion, committed a murder. And why? Because the mind of the one did not go with the act of the other.

Having referred at some length to the conversation of the accused with the Police, the Commissioner said he left the case to the jury. He earnestly impressed upon the jury to bear in mind that the prosecution were bound to provide their case beyond reasonable doubt, not fanciful doubt, but the strongest amount of suspicion, a suspicion which might be a clinging suspicion throughout the case, was not proof. If they thought the case was made out beyond reasonable doubt, in that case they must to their duty without flinching. If they thought a reasonable doubt existed in the case, their duty was equally clear, and prisoner was entitled to the benefit of it. He asked them to give the case their most serious consideration, and he prayed earnestly and reverently that they would be guided to the deliverance of a righteous verdict.

The jury left the Court to consider their verdict at 12.45, and while they were away another jury was empanelled to try another murder charge.[297]

297 Herbert Collins, a twenty-six year old mechanic, was treating some friends to a drive in his employer's car on the evening of 9 June 1906 when, on

When the members of this jury were sworn in, the Court was adjourned for half an hour for luncheon.

Twenty-five minutes later, before the return of the Commissioner, the jury came back into Court agreed upon their verdict. In absolute silence the Clerk of Assizes asked the foreman for their decision: in response he announced that they found the prisoner Not Guilty.

The announcement had comparatively little effect upon the accused, and although his face brightened he made no remark. His mother, who wore a light summer blouse and a bouquet of roses, and his father, who sat with her in the well of the Court, looked radiantly happy.

It was the accused's twenty-second birthday – another notable coincidence in this case of coincidences.

Mr Parfitt called attention to the fact that the jury has only returned a verdict on the indictment for the murder of Richard Phillips, but as only similar evidence could be offered on the indictment for the murder of Mary Phillips, the jury returned a formal verdict of Not Guilty in that case also…

There was considerable excitement in the vicinity of the Court when the jury's verdict was made known, and there was a large crowd of people in the street. Prisoner's father went out into the hall, but his mother remained in Court during the opening of the next case. In the hall Mr Taylor met the Town Clerk of Coventry, who was instructing counsel for the prosecution.

Smilingly accosting him, Mr Taylor said, "I congratulate you, sir." "Don't say that," replied Mr Sutton. "I have only done my duty."[298]

It was a suitably fitting present for Ernest Taylor on his birthday. But he would not celebrate for long; the Police were determined to

coming down a hill near Acock's Green, he struck cyclist Harold Price and knocked him to the ground. Price had foolishly been hanging on to a trailer being towed by a family member on a motorcycle, and had failed to see the car approaching. Collins failed to stop. Harold Price was taken to hospital, but died through his head wounds the following day. The Warwick jury found Collins Guilty of manslaughter and he was sentenced to nine months' imprisonment with hard labour. [Calendar of Prisoners 1868-1929, 1906, Warwickshire: Herbert Collins; *Gloucestershire Chronicle*, 16 June 1906; *Aberdeen Press and Journal*, 14 June 1906.]
298 *Leominster News*, 3 August 1906.

get their man, and brought forward an indictment for the burglary charge for which he had been originally arrested.

While Lord Coleridge agreed that the case could be heard that same day, the prosecution consented to the trial being held over to the Winter Assizes, and Taylor was taken down to await his second turn in the Warwick dock.[299]

Given he had just escaped the hangman's noose – not necessarily because he hadn't committed the foul murders of Richard and Mary Phillips, but because there was insufficient evidence to prove that he had done so – he must have felt good about his chances of beating the burglary charge as well.

299 *Leominster News*, 3 August 1906.

8

THE JUDGE'S SURPRISE

Ernest Taylor's optimism was unfounded.

Having spent a further five months in the Warwick cells, awaiting the start of the Winter Assizes, he was finally brought up to appear before Mr Justice Ridley[300] on Friday, 7 December 1906.

One newspaper helpfully reminded its readers that Taylor had been in prison since early January – almost an entire year – charged first with the burglary at his neighbours' house, then stealing a bicycle, and subsequently of double murder.[301]

As was the case with the murder trial, Robert and Ellen Taylor sat in the courtroom each day to support their son, who was once again defended by Mr H.H. Joy.

Mr Henry Maddocks prosecuted on behalf of Coventry Town Clerk George Sutton,[302] and laid out the evidence very clearly against Ernest Taylor.

A chain found among his possessions was the one stolen from Mrs Wilson, who had owned it for twenty years and recognised it at a glance. An unusual brace had been found in his carpenter's

---

300 Sir Edward Ridley was made a Justice of the High Court in 1897 and assigned to the King's Bench Division. The appointment was almost certainly a political one, being proposed by the Conservative Lord Hailsham, and was "greeted with horror". The *Law Journal* said that the appointment "can be defended on no ground whatsoever. It would be easy to name fifty members of the Bar with a better claim." Ridley resigned from the Bench in 1917. On his death in 1928, Sir Frederick Pollock wrote that Justice Ridley had been "by general opinion of the Bar the worst High Court judge of our time, ill-tempered and grossly unfair."

301 *Bristol Times and Mirror*, 10 December 1906.

302 *Kenilworth Advertiser*, 15 December 1906.

Mr Justice Ridley

shop at Jenner Street, along with bits which matched the holes drilled into the Wilsons' door in order to remove the section through which an enterprising hand had been passed. Candles were found in his workshop which matched one left behind at the neighbours' house on the night of the burglary.

Despite Mr Joy complaining that the case was wholly circumstantial – there being no proof that any of the items in his client's possession belonged to the Wilsons – it looked bleak, and the jury agreed. Without leaving the box they returned a verdict of Guilty.

Mr Justice Ridley then stunned those present – probably even the prosecution – by commenting, "I have heard enough. I know what sort of man this is. There is another charge against him [the theft of a bicycle]. He must go to penal servitude for fourteen years."[303]

As the Judge spoke there was a cry from the back of the barristers' seat, where prisoner's father and mother had been sitting throughout the case. The two rose from their seats, the mother crying loudly, and the father, waving his arms, shouted, "He is an innocent man." The mother, shaking her umbrella in the direction of the Judge, shouted, "He is innocent, everyone knows he is innocent."

His Lordship ordered the two to be removed from the Court.

Mr Taylor: "I can go out, but he is innocent."

The Judge: "I will have you committed to prison if you do not go."

Policemen went to Mr and Mrs Taylor, and pushed them out of the Court. The mother continued to cry out, "He is innocent," and used her umbrella freely as the constables got her out of the large waiting room. Mrs Taylor was in a hysterical condition, and

303 *Birmingham Daily Mail*, 7 December 1906.

continued to shout until she was in the street, to the consternation of the people who were assembled in the building.

The prisoner, who seemed completely staggered by the sentenced, was quickly removed from dock.

The severity of the sentence created a sensation in the Court, and it was some moments before quiet was restored. Outside the Court the sentence was the topic of animated conversation.[304]

Ernest Taylor was taken down to the Warwick cells. The charge against him of stealing the bicycle from outside the Hare and Hounds was allowed to sit on file.

The pronouncement of the heavy sentence might well have knocked the wind out of his sails, but he now had a long period of incarceration ahead of him in which to reflect on the truth of his part in the murders of Mary and Richard Phillips.

The pressure soon told; just weeks later, on 3 January 1907, he was taken to Hatton Lunatic Asylum for treatment[305] on what would prove to be the first instance of troubled mental wellbeing.

During his sojourn, his defending counsel prepared an appeal. As early as 13 December, the *Coventry Evening Telegraph* reported that Mr Masser was arranging for a petition to be drawn up, asking for a pardon on the grounds that the conviction ought to have been quashed; perhaps realising the unlikelihood of that coming to pass, as an alternative Masser called for a reduction of the sentence due to it being excessive.[306]

Masser also intended to tell the Home Secretary that Judge Ridley should not have taken into account the second charge, of stealing a bicycle, to which Taylor would have pleaded Not Guilty.[307]

The petition was presented by William Johnson, MP for Nuneaton, in the absence of Coventry's A.E.W. Mason.[308] Had Richard Phillips's favourite local politician supported an appeal for clemency on behalf of Ernest Taylor, the murdered man would no

304 *Kenilworth Advertiser*, 15 December 1906.
305 *Warwick and Warwickshire Advertiser*, 5 January 1907.
306 *Coventry Evening Telegraph*, 13 December 1906.
307 *Nuneaton Observer*, 14 December 1906.
308 *Coventry Evening Telegraph*, 19 February 1907.

Portland Prison.

doubt have turned in his grave.

A decision came soon enough. On 19 February 1907 it was reported that Home Secretary Herbert Gladstone had written to Mr Johnson to say that he could not grant a pardon; nor could he consider a reduction of sentence so soon after conviction.[309]

Now back at Warwick following his brief stay at Hatton Asylum, during which his health had markedly improved, Taylor was prepared for transfer to Portland Prison on the Dorset coast to continue his sentence. He left Warwick as Prisoner G628[310] on 9 March 1907, just three months into a long fourteen years.[311]

309 *Coventry Evening Telegraph*, 19 February 1907.
310 UK, Registers of Habitual Criminals and Police Gazettes, 1834-1934.
311 *Leamington Spa Courier*, 15 March 1907.

9.

WATER AND TRENCHES

Ernest Taylor seems to have spent his time quietly at Portland, not getting into any trouble nor giving the authorities reason to transfer him elsewhere.

Almost four years to the day since he arrived at the facility, the 1911 Census captured a snapshot of life at Portland at that moment.

There were 659 convicts, housed in cells across six halls, being monitored closely by just thirty-six officers. The Principal Warders were Jeremiah McElligott, Henry Prior, William Cordey and Henry Rosewarne, all aged between fifty-three and sixty-two, and vastly experienced.

Taylor is listed as being twenty-six years old, single, previously earning a living as a pattern maker and joiner.

His companions included fifty-seven year old George Bowles, about to end a four year sentence for arson; twenty-nine year old Arthur Bage, who helped himself to the silver proudly displayed at Peckham Methodist Church in 1906; and one-legged William Quirk, sentenced to seven years in 1909 for sexually assaulting a four year old girl.[312]

At some point within the next three years Taylor was transferred to Maidstone Prison, probably to prepare him for an early discharge. His apparent good behaviour was rewarded when he was released six and a half years early, having served just over half of his full term. He walked out of Maidstone Gaol on Friday, 29 May 1914

---

312 1911 Census; UK, Registers of Habitual Criminals and Police Gazettes, 1834-1934; *Edinburgh Evening News*, 12 September 1906; *Empire News & The Umpire*, 26 December 1909.

on special licence – a Ticket of Leave man. This meant that, while he was granted his freedom, it was under certain conditions. Ernest Taylor's licence expired on 5 December 1920 – the date his sentence would have been completed.

His physical appearance was recorded in the Habitual Criminals Register held at New Scotland Yard, to aid in identification should he re-offend: 5ft 7½in tall, dark brown hair with green eyes. He had a scar on his right temple, and was tattooed with a star and cross on his left forearm, and a tattooed ring on his wedding finger.

As was customary, his destination on release was also recorded. Taylor was sent to London, care of the Central Association.[313] Established in 1911, the Central Association for the Aid of Discharged Prisoners endeavoured to assist convicts on their discharge. The prisoner would be found a home, and work – in Ernest Taylor's case, as a carpenter.

He appears to have been placed at the Church Army Home, one of a number around the capital run by the charity founded by the Revd Wilson Carlile in 1882. The Homes were established six years later, with the intention of offering a fresh start to society's outcasts. Inmates earned their bed and board by carrying out work in their particular trade, and were encouraged to find employment outside of the charity, so that they might take the first step to rehabilitation.[314]

Despite apparently having all he needed to make a fresh start, Ernest Taylor was desperately unhappy. Just a week after his discharge from Maidstone Prison, he wanted to end it all.

What happened next was covered in detail by the press:

COVENTRY MAN IN TROUBLE IN LONDON

CHARGE OF ATTEMPTED SUICIDE

At the Thames Police Court, London, on Tuesday [25 June 1914], Charles Ernest Robert Taylor, of Coventry, was charged on remand with having attempted to commit suicide by throwing

313 UK, Registers of Habitual Criminals and Police Gazettes, 1834-1934.
314 See 'Care of Liberated Criminals' in *Catholic Encyclopedia Vol 12* (Chapter III: Modern Prison Reforms), 1913.

Interior of the Thames Police Court.

himself into the Thames on the night of June 13th.

It was stated at the previous hearing that at 10.30 on the night of June 13th, the prisoner walked into the Thames Police Station with his clothes saturated with water, and to the officer in charge he said, "I have been in the water. I walked in. I am tired of my life." He appeared to be very ill, and when taken into court he was remanded. In the interval he had improved in health, and the case was proceeded with.

A detective officer said the accused, on June 11th, reported himself as having just come out of prison after serving his term of penal servitude for burglary, his sentence having been passed in 1906. His licence did not expire until 1920. Another officer said the sentence was treated as one of ten years by the prison authorities.

The prisoner had no friends, and he was very depressed. An adjournment had previously been taken in the case for inquiry, the magistrate ordering the detention of the man in the prison infirmary with the remark that it would be better for him than wandering about the streets.

Certain papers were now handed to the magistrate without being ready in court.

Mr Leicester (to Taylor): "Have you anything to say?"

Taylor: "I am very sorry for what has occurred."

"What made you do it?" – "I was in difficulties."

"You won't get out of difficulties that way. What are you going to do when you get out of this trouble?" – "Well, I will do better."

"If I look over this will you promise not to do anything of the kind again?" – "Yes, Sir."

"I understand that the Church Army are willing to help you. Will you go back?" – "Yes, thank you, Sir."

The magistrate told Taylor they could not having him wandering about the streets and trying to kill himself. The Church Army were willing to help him in spite of what had occurred.

In binding Taylor over to be of good behaviour his Worship made it a condition that he should go back to the Church Army Home, and to this Taylor readily agreed.[315]

*

His movements over the next few years are sketchy. Later newspaper reports claimed that soon after his appearance before the London magistrates he enlisted with the Warwickshire Regiment, with the outbreak of the Great War, and was billeted in Northampton.[316]

With no available record of Ernest Taylor's military service, we are unable to say what happened to him. All we know is that his time in France was brief, for around six months after the Warwickshire Regiment landed in Normandy he was brought back to England suffering shell shock, and spent some months receiving treatment,

---

315 *Kenilworth Advertiser*, 27 June 1914.

316 *Northampton Chronicle and Echo*, 11 April 1922. There appears to be no trace of Ernest Taylor's military record. The Wartime Memories Project lists his probable service, giving the 7th Battalion Royal Warwickshire Regiment as a Territorial Force headquartered at Coventry, with their drill hall situated in Queen Victoria Road. The 7th Battalion was formed in October 1914, part of the Warwickshire Brigade, South Midland Division. They mobilised to the Northampton area in February 1915, then Chelmsford the following month. The formation became the 182nd Brigade, 61st (South Midland) Division in August 1915. They landed in France on 21 May 1916.

Royal Victoria Hospital at Netley.

first in the military's Royal Victoria Hospital at Netley, near Southampton,[317] and then Hatton Asylum.[318]

He then joined the Royal Flying Corps – again records are minimal – but was discharged before the end of the conflict, apparently due to his worsening mental condition.[319]

317 Construction of the Royal Victoria Hospital or Netley Hospital started in 1856, and the facility opened for patients in March 1863. It had 138 wards and around a thousand beds. It was used extensively during the Second Boer and First World Wars. The hospital fell into decline following WWII, and the facility closed in 1958 due to its high maintenance costs. Fire ravaged the building in 1963, and it was demolished three years later. A time capsule laid by Queen Victoria underneath the foundation stone was discovered; it contained a copy of the Hospital's plans, the first Victoria Cross, a Crimea Medal and coins of the realm.

318 *Coventry Herald*, 14 April 1922.

319 *Northampton Chronicle and Echo*, 11 April 1922. The pension application following Ernest Taylor's death states that he was removed from duty due to poor mental health.

10.

DON'T FORGET POOR MAGGIE

Before ending his association with the military, Ernest Taylor returned to the scene of happier times – to Northampton, where he had evidently met the woman with whom he would share the rest of his life.

Margaret Knibbs was just eight months older than Ernest. It seems the pair had met when he was billeted in Northamptonshire with the Warwickshire Regiment in 1914; she was a native of the county, at the time thirty-five years old. When Ernest was mobilised to the Western Front, Margaret was no doubt concerned about his welfare, awaiting his return. She had subsequently visited him at Hatton Asylum following his discharge through shell shock with her future father-in-law, Robert Taylor.[320]

The couple married a year after his release from Hatton, at Holy Sepulchre's at Northampton, on 22 December 1918. The Norman-period church was but a few moments' walk from the Knibbs family home of 23 Park Street, where both bride and groom were recorded as residing at the time of the happy event.

Ernest Taylor, aged thirty-four, was listed as being in the Royal Air Force; his new wife had no given occupation, but curiously had her age recorded as thirty-one, instead of the correct thirty-nine.[321]

Despite the lack of a profession on the certificate, earlier that year Margaret had been one of a number of women passing an

320 *Coventry Standard*, 15 April 1922.
321 Marriage certificate of Charles Ernest Robert Taylor and Margaret Knibbs.

examination by the St John Ambulance Association in Home Nursing at her hometown of Earls Barton.[322] It was clear that Margaret had a caring nature.

She had been born on 20 November 1879 at Dallington, a village close to Northampton, to farmer James Knibbs and his wife Sophia.[323] There were two older brothers, William and Charles.[324] Margaret was baptised on 1 February 1880.[325] James helped to run the farm belonging to his widowed father, seventy-eight year old William Knibbs.[326] Margaret's younger siblings Mary, Edward and George soon followed.[327]

Following his father's death in 1886[328] James Knibbs moved the family to Northampton, where daughter Edith was born at 160 Kettering Road in August 1886. By the time another daughter, Annie, arrived in 1889 James was working as a carrier, the family living at Earls Barton. Their home, on North Road, would be the family's sanctuary for more than a decade.[329]

The 1891 Census saw Margaret and her younger siblings at school. In September that year Winifred, the final child born to James and Sophia, arrived.[330]

Their children had grown by the turn of the Twentieth century; eldest son William was a professional soldier, Charles a grocer's porter. Margaret, now twenty-one years old, was a schoolteacher.[331]

By the 1911 census the family had moved to 23 Park Street, a comfortable terraced house comprising six rooms.[332] James was now sixty-six and Sophia sixty-four. Of their children, Margaret, Edward and Winifred were still at home. Margaret, now thirty-one, appears to have abandoned her teaching career and was recorded as

322 *Northampton Mercury*, 1 March 1918.
323 Birth certificate of Margaret Knibbs.
324 1881 Census.
325 Baptismal register.
326 1881 Census.
327 Baptismal records.
328 Probate record for William Knibbs.
329 Baptismal records.
330 Baptismal register.
331 1901 Census.
332 1921 Census.

The Horse and Jockey at the end of Park Street, Northampton.

earning a living by operating a cardboard box machine.[333]

Twenty-six year old Edward married Bertha Page in October that year, leaving Margaret and Winifred at home with their parents.[334]

It seems almost certain that Ernest Taylor moved into 23 Park Street at the time of his marriage to Margaret late in 1918. At the end of the street was the Horse and Jockey public house, which was no doubt frequented by Ernest. Beyond that, looming on the other side of Upper Mounts, was Northampton Prison. Even after all he had gone through since his release, Ernest Taylor was unable to escape his past.[335]

It was time for him to find a job. The well-established firm of builders A.L. and H.W. Chown of Northampton's Edinburgh Road had placed a series of advertisements offering newly-built

333 1901 Census.
334 Marriage certificate of Edward Knibbs and Bertha Page.
335 The over-populated Upper Mounts area of Northampton was redeveloped in the 1930s, with the site of HMP Northampton now being occupied by Mounts Baths. Should Ernest Taylor had been alive to witness these development works, he would no about have winced to observe his home on Park Street being replaced by a more modern courthouse and police station.

property in the town,[336] and helping hands were sought to help them cope with an expanding post-war business, especially new council housing in the suburbs which had been incorporated into the borough in 1901.[337]

The Northampton newspapers carried advertisements asking for tradesmen including carpenters and joiners to contact the company,[338] and it seems likely that Ernest Taylor responded to this appeal, for by the time of the 1921 Census eight months later he was recorded as working for A.L. and H.W. Chown, Builders and Contractors. He was a month shy of his thirty-seventh birthday.

But things had changed quickly at 23 Park Street. Whereas the house had been previously a hive of activity, the Census shows just Ernest and Margaret living there, along with her sister Edith. She was at the time a single thirty-four year old earning a living running a confectionery stand for Jones Bros, confectioners and jam manufacturers,[339] who had a base at Abington Square but had for many years supplied shops throughout Northampton.[340]

In 1920 a series of dramatic events had affected the Knibbs family. In the Spring, Winifred married Samuel Richards, the happy occasion no doubt enjoyed by all. But just two months later father James died; mother Sophia followed in the October.[341]

With just Ernest and Margaret now at the former Knibbs family home, inviting Edith to join them and help share the living costs would have made sense.

But in early 1922 Ernest Taylor work dried up with Chown, and he subsequently spent several weeks unemployed, sparking another period of depression.

---

336 For example, two houses in Kingsthorpe Grove advertised for sale in the *Northampton Chronicle and Echo*, 8 March 1920.

337 Founded by builder Henry Chown in the last days if the nineteenth century, the company continued building new estates into the 1980s.

338 See, for example, the *Northampton Daily Echo* of 24 August 1920.

339 1921 Census.

340 Advertisements for Jones Bros. appeared regularly in the Northampton newspapers from 1911 to 1931.

341 Marriage index; Death registers; *Northampton Chronicle and Echo*, 15 October 1920.

His father Robert, now seventy-four, knew all about these episodes – "When they came on, he was in a very bad state... he got it in his head that he would never be any good any more," he later said – and decided to go over to Northampton to see his son in an attempt to lift his spirits.

He arrived around midday on Tuesday 4 April, but Ernest was out at work, having secured short-term employment, so Robert sat with his daughter-in-law Margaret and waited. At 5.40pm Ernest came in, and seemed surprised to see his father. "Well, my lad, I've come over to have a look at you," he said, and the three of them had tea as Robert attempted to cheer up his son.[342]

Father and son had a chat, then went out for a couple of drinks. On returning back to No. 23 they sat talking for a little longer, before Robert went to bed at nine o'clock, telling Ernest he would see him in the morning.

Early the next day, before setting off for work, Ernest promised his father, "Well, Dad, if I can square up all right by Easter I shall cycle over and see you and mother."

Robert set off on the return journey to Coventry, expecting to see his son again soon, Easter being a little over a week away.

On the Friday, 7 April, Ernest Taylor had no work. Late in the morning he got his bike and told Margaret he was going out, but would not be long.[343]

She never saw him again.

At Coventry, Robert and Ellen were still living at 16 Spencer Street, the home Ernest Taylor had known since childhood.

At 8.30pm they were sitting together when they heard a rumbling at the letter-box of their front door.

Robert Taylor later said:

> I said to my wife, "Somebody's having a game with us, I should think." I did not go straight away as I thought it was some lads having a game, but when I did go to open the letter-box I found it full up to the bottom of the door. I pulled all the things out of

342 *Coventry Herald*, 14 April 1922.
343 *Coventry Standard*, 14 April 1922.

the letter-box and carried them to the kitchen table, where there was a light.

I found a pair of khaki gloves, wet through with the rain, then a piece of white rag with a watch and chain wrapped in it. My wife said, "Why, that's Ernest's chain," and I answered, "So it is." There was another piece of rag with 1s 8½d in it, and a soiled visiting card bearing [my son's] name and address and business, and on the back was scribbled in pencil:

> "Friday night.
> Dear Mother and Father.
> Cheer up, and forgive me.
> Don't forget poor Maggie.
> Love to all.
> Yours, C.E.R. Taylor.
> x x x x"

Ellen Taylor wondered aloud whether her son had travelled over on his bicycle, but Robert doubted it, saying he would have heard him had he done so. Yet when they looked outside the back door there was Ernest's bike, leaning against the kitchen window. There was no sign of their son.

The Taylors went back indoors, uncertain what to do. Some minutes later Robert decided to go to the Police station, fearful that Ernest's delicate mental state might see him come to harm. He gave a full description of what had happened to the officers on duty, and went back home to see if his son would return.

Robert Taylor stayed up all night waiting, to no avail, and the following morning went back to the Police station, and also to the Union Workhouse, but nobody had heard anything.

In Northampton, Margaret Taylor was also unsettled by her husband's disappearance, and began to make enquiries around their neighbourhood.

*

On the morning of Sunday, 9 April, forty year old John Over[344]

---

344 John Over was born in Coventry on 24 July 1881.

left his home of 23 Broadway, Earlsdon to take his dog for a walk,[345] and some much-needed peace and quiet. Although relatively late in life, he and wife Rose, thirty-nine,[346] had welcomed their first child, John Jr, eight days earlier.[347]

The couple had married at All Saints, Coventry on 30 June 1906[348] – while Ernest Taylor was languishing in Warwick Gaol awaiting his trial for the murder of Richard and Mary Phillips.

It was Rose's father, Samuel Arnold, whose death in mysterious circumstances was assessed by Dr Loudon in the August of 1906[349] – the infamous Samuel Arnold who had served a six-month prison sentence for the manslaughter of a man named John Plant during a bare knuckle boxing match on Hearsall Common in 1881.

Now, in 1922, life had moved on rapidly. Rose's sister, Alice Arnold, had been elected onto Coventry City Council three years earlier as the Worker's Union candidate, becoming one of Coventry's first two female councillors alongside the Labour candidate, Ellen Hughes.[350]

Following their marriage John and Rose had settled in Earlsdon, first at Broomfield Road[351] and then their long-standing home of 23 Broadway,[352] with John earning a living as a mechanic.

In the days following the birth of their son, an hour or two of peace and quiet was probably exactly what John Over needed. After an hour's walk along the Kenilworth Road he found himself at Gibbet Hill. It was a quarter to one.

Entering the coppice on the right-hand side of the road, his canine companion – whose name was sadly not recorded in subsequent

---

345 *Midland Daily Telegraph*, 10 April 1922.
346 Rose Arnold was born on 21st March 1883.
347 Date of birth of John Robert Over from 1939 Register.
348 Marriage certificate of John Over and Rose Arnold.
349 See page 106.
350 Alice would serve on the council for thirty-six years, and became Coventry's first female Mayor in November 1937. For a detailed examination of the lives of the Arnold family, see *The Watchmaker's Revenge* by Adam Wood (2021).
351 1911 Census.
352 1922 Census and 1939 Register.

Gibbet Hill c1920.

press reports – suddenly began to bark and become restless. Nearby, John noticed to his shock and horror, was the body of a man, hanging by the neck from a branch of a beech tree some eighteen feet from the ground. His feet were four feet from the earth.

Borrowing a knife from a man who had at that moment walked past, Mr Over cut the rope and gently laid the body to the ground.[353] It was immediately obvious the man was dead, with rigor mortis having set in, so John sent the passer by to fetch the Police from Kenilworth.

Inspector Joseph Hawkes[354] arrived, and examined the body of the dead man. He was lying on his back, with a short length of clothes line tied loosely around his neck – the rest was still tied

353 *Coventry Herald*, 14 April 1922.

354 Joseph Henry Hawkes was the son of a former Police Superintendent at Shipston on Stour, joining the Warwickshire Constabulary in 1906. After serving at Stratford Upon Avon, Rugby, Brinklow and Warwick, Hawkes was promoted inspector in December 1921 and took up residence at Kenilworth Police Station. He became ill in 1924, and passed away suddenly at the station on 29 August 1924 aged just thirty-eight. He was honoured with a large Police funeral. See obituary in the *Coventry Herald*, 5 September 1924.

firmly around the branch of the beech tree. Around the deceased's neck was an indentation which corresponded with the noose. It was clear the man had been dead for some time.

The inspector searched his clothing and found six printed business cards, which read:

C.E.R. Taylor
Carpenter and Joiner
23, Park Street, Northampton

On the reverse of one card was written, by hand, "God bless my dear wife," and on another, "16, Spencer Street, Coventry."

Warwickshire Constabulary Sergeant Cecil Pink[355] arrived and assisted Inspector Hawkes with removing the body to Bostock's Farm nearby, where it was placed in the motor-house to await a medical examination.[356]

Mr Bostock allowed his dairy farm[357] to be used as the venue for the inquest, and this took place at Gibbet Hill Farmhouse two days later, on the afternoon of Tuesday 11 April.

With Coroner for Warwickshire E.F. Hadow ill, the hearing was presided over by Deputy Coroner Dr W.R.W. Asplin who, after hearing of the events leading up to the discovery of the body, asked Robert Taylor about his son's treatment for shell shock. The response was harrowing:

---

355 Cecil H. Pink joined the Warwickshire Constabulary in March 1909, serving at several locations in the county including Stratford Upon Avon, Rugby and Nuneaton. He served several years during the Great War as detective sergeant at White and Poppe's munitions factory, following which he took charge of the Styvechale section for the Foleshill Division. He was promoted inspector in 1923 and returned to Nuneaton, where he celebrated twenty-six years in the Force in 1926. He finally retired two years later, and died in 1941. [*Midland Counties Tribune*, 2 April 1926; *Coventry Standard*, 3 May 1941.]

356 *Kenilworth Advertiser*, 15 April 1922.

357 When Mr E. Bostock sold his livestock in 1928, an advertisement in the *Warwick and Warwickshire Advertiser* of 18 August promoted an auction at Gibbet Hill Farm, Kenilworth, listing one hundred dairy shorthorns and sixteen well-bred bulls, including first prize Royal winner 'Streetaston Gold Prince II'.

Gibbet Hill Farmhouse

When they brought him from France his clothes were in an awful state – stiff with blood, but not his own, and they took him to hospital. He was there about three months, and then they took him under escort to Hatton Asylum, where he stayed about two months, and was discharged in 1917. He has been home time after time on visits to Spencer Street, but one or two of those occasions he has been very funny.[358]

Robert Taylor added that while Ernest was being treated at Hatton, he and Margaret had visited him in an attempt to cheer him up, and had done all they could to lift his spirits on the occasions he had acted strangely when visiting the family home.

Widow Margaret Taylor told the coroner that whenever a story had appeared in the newspapers about someone taking their own life, her husband had told her, "Well, Maggie, I shall never do anything like that" – having conveniently forgotten his own walk into the Thames back in 1914.[359]

358 *Coventry Herald*, 14 April 1922.
359 *Kenilworth Advertiser*, 15 April 1922.

She said that Ernest had been out of work for several weeks, and was worried because money was tight. At this Dr Asplin commented that, in those post-war years, many had been out of work for far longer periods, and asked Mrs Taylor if there were any large debts weighing over the couple. She failed to give a definite answer, but indicated there was not.[360]

Despite Margaret's denial, one newspaper claimed that, in later years, although now married and living at Northampton, Taylor

> had not forgotten Coventry, and sometimes came over to the city. He borrowed money several times of citizens, but generally paid his debts to the minute. Within a very recent period he tried to borrow a larger sum than usual, but did not succeed.[361]

With all the evidence heard, Deputy Coroner Asplin returned a formal verdict that the deceased had committed suicide whilst temporarily insane.

There is no certainty as to when Ernest Taylor ended his life. He had clearly been dead for some time before John Over discovered the swinging body, but had he headed straight to Gibbet Hill after forcing his belongings into his parents' letter-box on the Friday evening, or wandered around for several hours before arriving at the fatal spot late on the Saturday?

What had driven him to take his own life? Was it a prolonged bout of depression, initiated by the shell shock he took away from the Western Front and reignited when relatively minor problems such as money worries surfaced from time to time? This seems plausible, but the fact that he had tried to drown himself in the Thames following his release from prison and before his war service seems to point to his decade-long incarceration as the root of his low spirits.

Alternatively, had he, after all, been harbouring a guilty secret for all those years? The chance to finally learn the truth of Charles Ernest Robert Taylor's involvement in the murders of Mary and

---

360 *Coventry Herald*, 14 April 1922.
361 *Coventry Standard*, 14 April 1922.

Richard Phillips died with him on that beech tree at Gibbet Hill.

As one reporter put it: "His violent death at his own hands was the end of a troublesome life."[362]

362 *Coventry Standard*, 14 April 1922.

11.

AFTERMATH

In the immediate aftermath of Ernest Taylor's suicide the family attempted to pick up the pieces of their lives.

His widow – poor Maggie – applied to the authorities on 2 May 1922 asking for a pension based on Ernest's service with the Royal Flying Corps. Three months later, in August, she received a rather terse reply that she was ineligible, because she and Ernest had "married after [his] removal from duty on account of aggravation which caused death" – a clear reference to a long history of depression.[363]

What happened to Margaret in later years in uncertain. She may be the Margaret Taylor who died at Brackley, Northamptonshire in October 1960 aged seventy-eight; alternatively, she could be the Margaret Taylor who survived to the fantastic age of ninety-eight, passing away at Wellingborough in July 1979.[364]

Richard Phillips's sons Thomas and Wilfred, who had acted as his executors, both went on to live long and happy lives.

Thomas had married Laura Westwood in 1899. Later that year son Thomas Jr arrived, with daughter Annie being born in 1901.[365] The family were at the time living at Highfield Street (now Eld Road), with Thomas working as a motorcycle fitter.[366]

But by the next census, in 1911, the Phillips family were living

363 UK, WWI Pension Ledgers and Index Cards, 1914-1923.
364 Death registers.
365 Marriage and Birth indexes.
366 1901 Census.

in Sheffield. Thomas was manager of a garage, repairing motorcars. This was a highly skilled career, at a time when there were only an estimated 14,000 vehicles being produced each year.[367]

This period of technological advancement was mirrored in the air, for the Great War soon broke out. Thomas's son Thomas Jr, although still a student, enlisted into the Royal Air Force on 12 November 1917, and was appointed an Air Cadet six months later. While he would not see any action, and was in fact discharged in July 1918 – the war coming to an end – his grandfather Richard would no doubt have been both proud of his grandson's achievements, and the fact that he had almost engaged in aerial combat would have seemed incredible to a man born in 1829. On his discharge papers Thomas Phillips Jr was recorded as being eighteen years old, 5ft 3¼ inches tall, with a thirty-two inch chest, and brown hair.[368]

At the outbreak of the Second World War, and the taking of the National Register of 1939, Thomas Sr was still in Sheffield, and still working as a car fitter. He was now seventy-four years old, and wife Laura seventy-three.[369]

At some point in the few decade Laura passed away – she cannot be found in records – and Thomas returned to the Midlands. He died in Birmingham in 1951, aged eighty-six.[370]

Outliving Thomas by two years was brother Wilfred Phillips. He had married Alice Westwood in April 1900 – a year after his brother Thomas had married Alice's sister Laura – and nine months later daughter Alice Jr arrived. The family were then living at 68 Broad Street, Coventry, with Wilfred earning a living as a cycle and motor car engineer. Little Alice was just days old when the enumerator for that year's census knocked on their door.[371]

Ten years later the family had moved to No. 176 Broad Street, with Wilfred now employed as a chargehand at an ironworks and

---

367 See *The Motor Men* by Peter King (1989).
368 UK, Royal Air Force Airmen Records, 1918-1940, Pieces 0901-1050 : 987 – Thomas Phillips.
369 UK National Register, 1939.
370 Death index.
371 1901 Census.

wife Alice bringing extra money into the household by working at a motor engine works.[372] They had at some point had a second child, who had sadly died before the time of the 1911 Census.

Wilfred and Alice continued to live in Coventry. He died in 1953.[373]

Thomas and Wilfred's elder brother Charles, the other of the three surviving children, had followed his father's choice of career and had worked as a watch repairer.[374] He had married Emma Marson in Coventry in 1886, and the couple soon moved to Ludlow, in Shropshire, where children Minnie[375] and Walter[376] soon arrived. Charles and Emma later adopted Emily Williams,[377] whose parents had died soon after her birth in 1899. Charles Phillips died in 1916 aged just fifty-four.[378]

Richard Phillips was, therefore, a grandfather to seven children at the time of his death.

The husband of his only daughter, John Jackson, remarried four years after Mary Ann's death, to Miriam Worrall. A daughter, Phyllis, arrived the following year.[379]

Reader, spare a thought for Rose Over. Her uncle, Oliver Style, had gone on a rampage around Coventry with a revolver, serving twenty years for the attempted murder of his wife. The following year, Rose's father killed a man while taking part in a bare knuckle boxing match on Hearsall Common. Her mother Caroline, Style's sister, died a slow and agonising death from syphilis.[380]

And then, just as she finally began to enjoy her own life in a comfortable home with her husband and newborn son, her husband

372 1911 Census.
373 Death index. There appears to be no record of Alice Phillips's passing.
374 1911 Census.
375 1888-1956.
376 1889-1968.
377 1897-1986.
378 Marriage, Birth and Death Registers.
379 Ibid.
380 These incidents are described in *The Watchmaker's Revenge* by Adam Wood (2021). See www.WatchmakersRevenge.com

John headed out on an innocent dog walk and discovered the body of a man hanging from a tree.

Rose would have been forgiven for wondering what she had done to deserve it all.

The horrific double murder was relegated to the 'Down Memory Lane' columns often seen in local newspapers. One such account, published in 1938, appeared under the byline 'Coventry Murder Stories', and was titled 'The Mystery of Stoke Park':

> In circumstances which indicated gross brutality an elderly couple, Mr and Mrs Phillips, of Hawthorn Cottage, Stoke Park, Coventry, were found murdered in their bedroom on January 13, 1906.
>
> The discovery started a train of events as bizarre as the murder most foul, which ended only in April, 1922, when Charles Ernest Robert Taylor, a cousin of the murdered pair, who had been acquitted on a charge of wilful murder at Warwick Assizes, was found hanging from a tree on the very spot where the gallows had stood on Gibbet Hill, Kenilworth Road, in bygone years.
>
> Many there were, old residents of Coventry who, reading of this second tragedy, harked back to the first, long days before the war, and shook their heads knowingly…
>
> Thief he was. Murderer? – perhaps. There are many who think today that with [Ernest] Taylor died the secret of the 'Stoke Park Murder'.[381]

*

At Stoke Park itself, crime occasionally reared its head. Three years after the murders, 'Glendene' – the home of Mary Phillips's friend Mrs Frances Mortimer – was burgled by a young man named Edward Stebbings, later described by newspapers as "a fresh complexioned, fair-haired youth, roughly dressed, and without a collar". Charles Mortimer had several items stolen in the raid, which took placed on 21 May 1909, including clothing and gold cufflinks.[382]

381 *Coventry Herald*, 2 April 1938.
382 *Coventry Evening Telegraph*, 24 May 1909.

Excitement was stirred when it was decided not to pursue a conviction, it being revealed that Stebbings had already been arrested for stealing four pairs of boots belonging to Henry Nicks, the Superintendent of the Boys' Labour Home at Warwick,[383] just eight days earlier.

The court at Warwick heard that Stebbings had previous, being bound over in November 1905 and February 1906 for suspected burglary at London, and receiving twelve months' imprisonment for finally being caught in the act in November 1907. He had clearly left the capital to try his luck in Coventry.

The young burglar pleaded Guilty at Warwick on 4 June 1909, and was sentenced to another twelve months' with hard labour.[384]

Edward Stebbings obviously was undeterred by the threat of imprisonment; in October 1910, just six months after his release, he was back in London and back in court. He was found Guilty of yet another burglary, this time under the alias of 'William Arrowsmith', and received eighteen months.[385]

*

Hawthorn Cottage, the scene of the tragedy, lost its name within days of the murders, becoming Beulah House. Robert Waterfall's grand greenhouse, in which he spent six years cultivating his tomatoes, was torn down in a matter of days. The plot of land between the cottage and Stoke Green which Mary Phillips owned, deliberately keeping empty to preserve the splendid view across the Binley Road, was sold along with the property and the murder house became obscured from view, nestled among the larger properties which had begun to spring up around the estate.

In the coming years a number of residents came and went.

In 1915 advertisements appeared in the *Coventry Evening Telegraph* placed by the then occupant offering a motorcycle for

---

383 *Leamington, Warwick, Kenilworth & District Daily Circular*, 16 June 1909.
384 UK Calendar of Prisoners 1868-1929: Edward Stebbings.
385 UK Registers of Habitual Criminals and Police Gazettes, 1834-1934: William Arrowsmith.

sale at the bargain price of £13;[386] two years later an "experienced, trustworthy" gentleman named Armour living at Beulah House appealed via the same newspaper over a number of weeks for a "post of responsibility".[387]

In October 1919 Magistrates Burbidge and Gregory heard that the then resident, a fitter named John Rushton, had been caught riding a bicycle at night without lights – an incident reminiscent of the events of 1906;[388] and in 1928, moving with the times, then resident Reginald Mayo was fined £1 for having no rear light on his Morgan Runabout,[389] a lightweight chassis driven by a motorcycle engine.

Before 1931 the house had been renamed 'Lyndhurst', and in February that year Cecil Wagstaff, the present incumbent who was employed in the council's Rates Office, was fined 20s for inconsiderately parking his car on Hay Lane and causing an obstruction for two hours and five minutes.[390]

In 1944 the house was offered up for sale by auction; it was available freehold, cold and empty. At the Hare and Squirrel hotel on Cow Lane, auctioneer James Martin oversaw bidding which reached £850 – perhaps a reasonable sum, given the sale was held deep into the war years.[391]

At some point the residence lost its identity, instead gaining a number as one of several properties lining what became known as South Avenue, as the estate became more populated and the former simple paths were properly paved to become roads.

It still stands today.

386 *Coventry Evening Telegraph*, 26 November 1915.
387 *Coventry Evening Telegraph*, 8 May 1917; 9 May 1917; 19 July 1917.
388 *Coventry Standard*, 3 October 1919.
389 *Coventry Evening Telegraph*, 26 July 1928.
390 *Coventry Evening Telegraph*, 2 February 1931.
391 *Coventry Evening Telegraph*, 26 February 1944; 11 March 1944.

WAS ERNEST TAYLOR GUILTY?

Despite his acquittal, was Charles Ernest Robert Taylor guilty of the Stoke Park murders?

The finger of guilt seems to point at him for so many reasons: his apparent identification by Benjamin Taylor and John Bonehill, who both had no hesitation in confirming he was the man they saw soon after it was believed the murders were committed, is difficult to explain away.

That he traded in bicycle parts was not disputed, and the so-called Stoke Lamp was proved to belong to a stolen machine whose parts found their way into Taylor's workshop. And his growing money worries gave a strong motive for a burglary-gone-wrong scenario.

This is strong evidence, albeit circumstantial, and that's why his defence counsel did a good job on casting enough doubt in the minds of the jury as to his guilt as to murder. There were surely few people inside the courtroom who truly believed Taylor to be innocent, yet absolute proof was not forthcoming.

For that reason alone, it has to be said that Ernest Taylor was lucky. But despite escaping the hangman's noose, he was condemned to a life of difficulty. The Police were determined they should get their man; the fourteen years awarded for the burglary charge allowed them to feel some measure of justice being served.

After serving a portion of his sentence, Taylor subsequently spent the final eight years of his short life under a dark cloud of mental illness. Even before experiencing the horrors of war which left him shell-shocked he had attempted to take his own life; that he eventually carried out the act despite apparently finding happiness with a loving wife indicates a troubled mind. Just what was the case of this long-standing depression?

And what are we to make of his cryptic comment that "the other is a married man with five children. If I suffer for it, he will thank me for it some day."

This certainly sounds like confirmation that a second man had been with Ernest that moonlit morning, as testified by Benjamin Taylor.

Ernest's father, Robert Taylor, reacted with fury when his namesake Benjamin pointed the finger at him at the inquest, outright calling the witness a liar. He and wife Ellen certainly made a big show of telling anyone who would listen that their son was innocent, and that Robert Taylor himself had been tucked up in bed long before the time it was suggested Richard and Mary had met their end. And, of course, the man cryptically referred to by Ernest had five children.

But what the court didn't hear – and was never reported in the newspapers covering the case – was that Robert Taylor had been married before, and had more children in addition to Ernest.

Growing up in the watchmaking area of Coventry,[392] despite his father William working as a dyer, Robert had married Betsy Glover, the daughter of watchmaker Henry Glover and his wife Jane,[393] at Holy Trinity on 3 September 1866. Both were nineteen years old.[394]

The bride had been born on 29 March 1846 to Henry and Jane,[395] the third of six children, and grew up first in Radford and then on West Orchard, where she was living when she met Robert Taylor.

A son, William – presumably named after Robert's father – was born on 18 June 1869,[396] and two years later the young family were

---

392 Census returns show Robert Taylor and his family at Junction Street in 1851 and York Street ten years later.
393 Baptismal record of Betsy Glover, 12 February 1860. She had been born on 29 March 1846.
394 Marriage certificate of Robert Taylor and Betsy Glover, witnessed by her brother Harry and sister Ellen.
395 Baptismal record of Betsy Glover.
396 Baptismal record of William Taylor.

living at Moat Street,[397] back in the watchmaking district, and son Robert Jr was born there later that year.[398]

Over the following decade three further children joined the family – Henry (b1873), Ada (1878) and Edith (1880).[399]

The 1881 Census captured the Taylor family living at Lower Wellington Street, Hillfields. They were still living there when another son, Frank, was born on 9 January the following year.[400]

But what should have been a happy time for the Taylors turned into a nightmare, when Betsy was stricken with what we would recognise today as post-natal depression.

The *Coventry Herald* of 22 September 1882 reported some sad news:

SAD CASE OF SUICIDE.

On Tuesday evening, at the Buck and Crown, Radford, an adjourned inquest was held before the Deputy Coroner (Mr S.R. Masser), touching the death of Betsy Taylor, aged thirty-seven,[401] wife of Robert Taylor, carpenter, Wellington Street, Coventry.

It appeared from the evidence that deceased had been in a very low state of mind for the past eight months, since the birth of her last child. She was constantly under the delusion that she had an internal cancer, and had apprehensions that her end was approaching. Although she had consulted several medical men respecting her condition, all of whom told her she had nothing to fear, she still persisted in her belief.

At length, under the advice of friends, she was taken to the Union [Workhouse Infirmary], where she recovered somewhat. On coming out again she went to live with her mother Mrs Jane Glover, Summer Row, Radford,[402] for a short time, after which she returned home and lived with her husband. She paid constant visits to her mother, however, after leaving her house.

---

397 1871 Census.
398 Baptismal record of Robert Taylor.
399 Baptismal records.
400 1939 Register.
401 *Sic*: She was thirty-five.
402 No. 14, according to the 1881 Census.

The Buck and Crown, Radford, where the inquest
into Betsy Taylor's death was held.

On Friday last [15 September 1882] the deceased purchased from Mr Welton, chemist, Bishop Street, a 3d packet of Battle's vermin killer, stating that she wanted it for killing mice, and giving the name of Mrs Taylor, 29 Spon Street. She then proceeded to her mother's house, and appeared to be in a very bewildered state of mind.

At about a quarter past three the mother left the house to go to the Spring, being away about ten minutes, and leaving deceased in the house alone. Deceased then accompanied her sister-in-law to her house,[403] where she was seized with violent convulsions of the limbs. It was believed she had taken poison, and the deceased herself made an admittance to that effect.

In about a quarter of an hour she died, evidently in great pain. Dr Read was summoned, but he did not arrive till after her death. He made a superficial examination of the body, and afterwards a post mortem at the Hospital. From these examinations he was of opinion that death has resulted from poisoning by strychnine, and he considered that a 3d packet off Battle's vermin killer contained sufficient of that poison to cause death.

403 Hannah Glover, who had married Betsy's brother William. The couple lived at 4 Summer Row. [1881 Census.]

The jury returned a verdict that the deceased had committed suicide whilst in an unsound mind.

The death was formally registered on 20 September 1882, when the inquest certificate was supplied by Deputy Coroner S.R. Masser.[404]

Did Masser remember the Taylor family, twenty years later, when he acted as defence solicitor for Ernest, and feel sympathy for all they had gone through?

Robert Taylor didn't remain alone for long. On 4 August 1883, less than a year after Betsy's sad passing at just thirty-five, he married Ellen Mary Elizabeth Dillow at St Thomas's on the Butts. He was at the time living in the watchmaking community that otherwise filled Hertford Square; still working as a carpenter and joiner, he was probably one of the few not working in the watchmaking trade.[405]

Ellen was recorded on the marriage certificate as living at Chapelfields; she had been employed as cook at the household of Rowland Hill, the renowned watchmaking and motor engineering employer who lived at 1 Hearsall Terrace,[406] and who would in time serve as a magistrate at her son's initial hearing.

The new Mrs Taylor assumed care of her husband's children. Their own son, Charles Ernest Robert, arrived on 26 July 1884. He was born at the new family home of 16 Spencer Street, which would prove to be the Taylors' sanctuary for over forty years. The new addition to the family was registered by his father on 5 August 1884.[407]

With the older children flying the nest by the time of the 1901 Census, only Frank and Ernest remained at home – although just the youngest was living with his parents on 10 January 1906, when Richard and Mary Phillips were murdered in their bedroom.

Of Robert's older children, William followed his father into the

---

404 Death certificate of Betsy Taylor.
405 Marriage certificate of Robert Taylor and Ellen Dillow. She was born in Warwick in 1853 to William, an agricultural labourer, and wife Ellen. She was thirty years old at the time of her marriage to Robert Taylor.
406 1881 Census.
407 Birth certificate of Charles Ernest Robert Taylor.

carpentry business. He married Alice and the couple had three children: William (b1894), Sydney (1895) and Alice Jr (1898).[408] He died in 1937, aged sixty-eight.[409]

Robert Taylor Jr married Anne Johnson at Brockton, Massachusetts, USA, on 23 November 1894.[410] The couple had one son, Stanley, born in Coventry in 1900. Also inheriting his father's talent, Robert earned a living as a wood turner.[411] He appears to have remained in America while Annie and Stanley travelled to and from their homeland more than once. He was living at Philadelphia in October 1906,[412] three months after his brother's trial for murder. Robert had died by the time his wife and son travelled aboard the liner RMS *Lusitania* when it was torpedoed by a German U-Boat on 7 May 1915, with five hundred passengers being killed – including Annie Taylor.[413] Fifteen year old Stanley survived and became a railway porter.[414] He died on 15 October 1973.[415]

Henry Taylor, third son of Robert and Betsy, avoided the temptation of the following the family trade and became a baker. He married Harriett Merry in 1899, and two years later was working as a breadmaker.[416] The couple had no children, but lived long lives; Henry had retired by the time of the 1939 Register, in which he is recorded as a retired baker. He and Harriett were then living at Bolingbroke Road. Henry died in 1953 aged eighty; Harriett lived to the grand age of ninety, passing away in 1966.[417]

Eldest daughter Ada was recorded in the 1901 Census as a

---

408 1911 Census.
409 Death Index.
410 Massachusetts, Marriage Records, 1840-1915.
411 1901 Census.
412 List of Alien Passengers for the US Immigration Officer at Port of Arrival, October 1906.
413 Probate record of Annie Sarah Taylor, which states she was a widow at the time of her death.
414 1939 Register.
415 Probate record of Stanley Robert Taylor.
416 Marriage register; 1901 Census.
417 Death registers.

domestic servant, employed in the household of watch manufacturer Samuel Wootton at 12 Cope Street. She died, unmarried, in 1910.

Sister Edith also died early; at just nineteen, early in 1900.[418]

The youngest son of Robert and Betsy, Frank, became a house painter and decorator. He was following that line of work by the time of the 1901 Census, which showed him living at Spencer Street with his father Robert and stepmother Ellen, as well as his half-brother Ernest.

Frank married Leah McKnight in the summer of 1905 and the couple moved into their own accommodation; a son, Frank Jr, was born at the end of 1906.[419]

The census of 1911 captured the family at 27 Vecqueray Street, Coventry, with Frank now twenty-nine and still working as a house painter. Leah was contributing by taking in work as a tailoress.

Another son, Horace, was born in 1914. In 1921 he was at full-time education, with elder brother Frank Jr, now fourteen, apprenticed to building company A. Matts & Son. His grandather Robert would have been proud – a chip off the old block.

The family were still at Vecqueray Street when Leah died on 17 January 1933 aged fifty.[420] Six years later, her widowed husband Frank was still at the long-standing address, and still working as a house painter.[421]

He eventually passed away in November 1944, aged sixty-one.[422]

*

Ernest Taylor cryptically told officers following his arrest that "the other" man involved was married with five children, but refused to divulge any information as to his identity.

Of his father's seven children – six with first wife Betsy, one with Ellen – daughter Ethel had died in 1900, and son Robert Jr had

---

418 Ibid.
419 Marriage and Birth records.
420 Probate record of Leah Taylor.
421 1939 Register.
422 Death register.

emigrated to America. At the time of the Stoke Park murders in 1906, therefore, Robert Taylor had five children close by – just as Ernest had claimed.

Was Benjamin Taylor right all along when he insisted that he was the older man of the two he had seen on the Binley Road minutes after the murders?

Robert Taylor lived to the age of eighty-five. He died of heart failure at the Gulson Road Hospital on 20 January 1933 – three days after his daughter-in-law Leah – with his home address registered as still being 16 Spencer Street. He had lived there for at least fifty years. Robert's demise was registered the following day by his son William, by then aged sixty-four.[423]

Wife Ellen followed six months later, on 21 July 1933, also at the Gulson Road Hospital. She too had suffered heart disease, but in her case she had also been stricken by rheumatoid arthritis. Her passing was registered the same day by her stepson Henry, Robert's second surviving son.[424]

Back in 1906, when her only son Ernest had just been sentenced to fourteen years' for burglary, she had hysterically protested his innocence while swinging her umbrella at court officers.

Did Ellen Taylor know more than she let on?

*

423 Death certificate of Robert Taylor, registered 31 January 1933.
424 Death certificate of Ellen Mary Elizabeth Taylor, registered 21 July 1933.

The final Coventry Races meeting at what became Stoke Park was held in March 1849.

Given what was to come, the result of the prestigious Craven Stakes steeplechase was a chilling premonition of events fifty-seven years later.

The winner, by three lengths, was Lord Chesterfield's horse The Victim – ridden to victory by a jockey named Taylor.[425]

425 *Lloyd's Weekly Newspaper*, 18 March 1849. The Victim went on to be one of the fancied runners in the 1850 Grand National, once again ridden by William Taylor, but failed to finish. The following year both horse and jockey fell at the National, with Taylor suffering a broken collarbone.

TIMELINE OF ERNEST TAYLOR

1884

26 July — Born at 16 Spencer Street, Coventry to Robert and Ellen Taylor.

1901

April — Working as a carpenter alongside his father.

1905

c January — Apprenticed to Mr Duggins.

c April — Set up in business for himself.

September — Asks engineer Tom Eales to make two metal 'scrapers' with curved ends.

16 September — A bicycle is stolen from John Lamont.

13 November — Bicycle stolen from William Green.

1906

1 January — Agrees to buy furniture from Charles Furnival; goes next day to admit he can't pay.

3 January — Breaks into next door neighbours' house.

4 January — Repairs neighbours' door, charging for the work.
Announces he is engaged to be married.
Visits Rose and Woodbine on Stoney Stanton Road, buys drinks with farthings stolen during the burglary.

10 January — Afternoon: visits Alma Inn on Stoney Stanton Road, tries to pay with farthings. A revolver he is carrying is confiscated by the landlord.
6.30pm: Arrives at Franks' Weaving Factory, West Orchard. Appeared to have been drinking.

	c7.00pm: Possibly the man who visited an ironmonger on Jordan Well, asking for an unsual wick to be inserted in a bicycle lamp.
	c7.10pm: Drinking at the Woolpack, Spon Street. Told to leave at 10.15pm. 10.25pm: Visits friend Charles Jordan at Cross Cheaping, leaves at 11.00pm.
11 January	4.20am: Benjamin Taylor sees two men on Binley Road; they flee when they become aware of his presence, one into Stoke Park and the other up a foothpath. He later identifies them as Ernest Taylor and his father Robert. 4.30am: Jone Boneham sees a man who has just emerged from the foopath leading from Binley Road. He later identifies him as Ernest Taylor. 6.30am: Arrives home via kitchen door; tells parents he has spent the night in the Jenner Street workshop. 7.30am: Visits Alma and asks for his revolver to be returned; told it is at the Police station.
17 January	Assists his father in their roles as undertakers at the funeral of Mary and Richard Phillips at London Road Cemetery.
19 January	Attends Coventry Police station asking for revolver. Questioned about the Spencer Street burglary; detained in custody.
27 January	Charged with burglary.
2 February	William Green attends Police, station and identifies a frame found in Taylor's workshop as being from his bicycle stolen in September 1905.
22 February	John Lamont attends Police station and identifies a frame sold by Ernest Taylor in November 1905 as being from his bicycle stolen two months earlier. He also identifies the Stoke Lamp found at Hawthorn Cottage as being from his machine.
10 March	Charged with murder.
19 March	Magistrates' hearing opens. Later committed to trial at Warwick Summer Assizes.
23 July	Trial opens.
26 July	Found Not Guilty.
7 December	Tried for burglary; sentenced to fourteen years' penal servitude.

1907

3 January	Sent to Hatton Lunatic Asylum for treatment.
9 March	Sent to Portland Prison, Dorset.

c1912   Transferred to Maidstone Prison, Kent.

1914

29 May	Released on Ticket-of-Leave after serving six years.
25 June	Appears before London magistrates after attempting to drown himself in the Thames.
c. September	Enlists in Warwickshire Regiment, billeted at Northampton.

1917   Discharged from Army due to shell shock; Sent to
Royal

Victoria Hospital at Netley, then Hatton Asylum.

1918

22 December	Marries Margaret Knibbs at Northampton.

1922

4 April	Visited at Northampton by father Robert Taylor.
7 April	Last seen by wife Margaret.
9 April	Found hanging at Gibbet Hill, Kenilworth.
11 April	Inquest returns verdict of 'Suicide whilst temporarily insane'.

BIBLIOGRAPHY

PRIMARY SOURCES

The National Archives
'Criminal depositions and case papers: MURDER: Taylor'
  (ASSI 13/36)

Other Archives
Non-Conformist and Non-Parochial Registers, 1567-1936,
  Piece 2980: Coventry, Vicar Lane (Independent), 1806-1837
UK Calendar of Prisoners
UK, Registers of Habitual Criminals and Police Gazettes
UK, Royal Air Force Airmen Records, 1918-1940
UK, WWI Pension Ledgers and Index Cards, 1914-1923

Other Primary Sources
1939 Register; Baptism records; Birth records; Census returns
  1841–1921; Marriage records; Death records

SECONDARY SOURCES

Newspapers, Journals and Directories
Aberdeen Press and Journal
Atherstone, Nuneaton and Warwickshire Times
Birmingham Daily Gazette
Birmingham Daily Gazette
Birmingham Gazette and Express

Birmingham Journal
Birmingham Mail
Bristol Times and Mirror
Coleshill Chronicle
Coventry Evening Telegraph
Coventry Herald
Coventry Observer
Coventry Standard
Coventry Times
Daily News
Edinburgh Evening News
Empire News & The Umpire
England & Wales, Criminal Registers
Gloucestershire Chronicle
Kenilworth Advertiser
Leamington Spa Courier
Leamington Spa Courier
Leamington, Warwick, Kenilworth & District Daily Circular
Leominster News
Lloyd's Weekly Newspaper
London Road Cemetery Burial Registers
Midland Counties Tribune
Midland Daily Telegraph
Northampton Chronicle and Echo
Northampton Daily Echo
Northampton Mercury
Nuneaton Advertiser
Rugby Advertiser
'Stoke Park, Coventry': a history compiled by Stoke Park
    Residents' Group
Warwick and Warwickshire Advertiser
Western Daily Press
White & Co.'s Commercial & Trades Directory of Birmingham
White's Directory and Gazeteer of Warwickshire

INDEX